The
Whirling Dance

Libby Sears Blair

Far From Walden Pond Publishing

Cover Art: Chad Waits

ISBN-13: 978-0692562659

ISBN-10: 0692562656

Published by Far From Walden Pond Publishing

Psalm 30:11-12, The Message

You did it: you changed wild lament
    into whirling dance;
You ripped off my black mourning band
    and decked me with wildflowers.
I'm about to burst with song;
    I can't keep quiet about you.
God, my God,

    I can't thank you enough.

For my two sweet girls, may you dance a beautiful dance all your days. Know that I love you with all my heart.

And for Keith who knows me decked in wildflowers. I am so grateful for you. I love you.

CONTENTS

CHAPTER ONE

I'm not ever sure what the actual calendar number is but I will always know when it happened. It was the night before Thanksgiving when my world was forever altered. That evening I was acutely aware of the significance of the events. This horrible thing was happening.

I know that everyone experiences some horrible thing in his or her life. Some experience more horrible things than others but these things are part of the very breath and life that we are granted. You can insert your own horrible thing where I am discussing my horrible thing. My horrible thing was the beginning of the end of my marriage. Sure, I know that divorces are a dime a dozen these days, but all who know me know that I experienced an out of the ordinary "horrible thing"(s) in the beginning of the end. It wasn't your average "We fell out of love", or "I have found another". As horrible as those things are (and I'm not discrediting any pain anyone has endured in a divorce), my horrible thing was one I couldn't even fathom. It was public to the point that it was on the evening news and in the state papers and had gone viral in the small town in which we lived. I will leave it at that out of respect for my children's father because ultimately, the good news is that the horrible thing became just a thing. The beginning was unbearable, truly. The middle was fuzzy and the end was oh, so clear.

I remember when I found out about the horrible thing. It was the night before Thanksgiving and I was home alone with the girls. I had let them stay up late that night because it was a holiday break from school. My oldest, Melody had already fallen asleep. She is an early riser so naturally, she had fallen asleep first. Anna was still up, so when I found out about the horrible thing, she witnessed me fall apart. Somehow in my trembling, in my utter despair as events were unfolding, I was aware that she was watching me fall apart. I had just enough mental capacity, since I was almost fully operating on emotions, on heartbreak, to call a friend to come to my side. I remember when my friend arrived my thought was that I couldn't believe this was happening on a holiday eve, a time that would always be marked with the blood of my heart. That's how it initially felt. It felt as though a knife had cut my heart out of my body. Why couldn't it have happened on say, March 7th? What's the memory in that date? I suppose that no matter when horrible things happen we etch in stone some remembrance of it and for me, at that moment, it was the night before Thanksgiving. I think I thought about the date during that time because my horrible thing was so huge and I knew my life was in pieces. Two hours prior, at eight o'clock it was fine and then by ten o'clock, it was never the same again.

Before the beginning of the end, this was my life: I was a wife. I had been married almost eleven years to my college sweetheart, Michael Ray. He was a physical education teacher, track coach and football coach at the local high school. We lived in Small Town, USA. At that time our daughters were five and eight years old. Anna was in her first year of school, in Kindergarten and Melody Grace was in the third grade. I had just ended a career as a Child Protective Services Social Worker and had begun my Masters of Arts in Special Education. My job as a Social Worker left me depleted daily of emotion and life.

Being a Social Worker was probably the best job I have ever had. I was good at it. I cared about people, namely children and their well-being, so naturally I took my job very seriously. For the most part, I had great relationships with so very many people that I encountered in the field such as therapists, lawyers, judges, law enforcement, clerk's offices, city, county and school officials. I worked many long hard hours to ensure that children were in safe homes in the event that they had experienced domestic violence, substance abuse, mental health issues or abuse and neglect. I worked with parents to fix the problems in their home and to get back on track for the sake of their children. In the event that they were not able or did not care to reunite with their children, I worked very diligently, sometimes in tears and sweat to find another home for the children. It was an exhausting and rewarding occupation. It took everything I had to do that job daily the way that it should be done. One in that occupation could never truly do enough.

I found that I could not continue to do that job and adequately meet the needs of my family. The last straw was an ice storm that occurred in 2009. Only a few of us were able to get to work during the week of the storm. This was the kind of storm that shut down half of the state. Many were without electricity for days and days. I reported to work and was told by my superiors that another social worker and I needed go do home visits and check on children without electricity. So as the Joan of Arcs that we were, we set out in her Chevy Equinox and went into the remotest part of the county to check on some children, all the while our own children were at home with their fathers fighting the ice and lack of heat. Going out was against our better judgment, but we had a job to be done. We were even told by our friends in law enforcement to be careful, that it was best that we not go; however, we were told by our superiors with in state government that we needed to check on the children. What a conundrum. We drove about ten miles out into the county just fine before we hit hills. Since we had gone ten miles, we had developed a little confidence and began to continue. We made it up a hill just fine, but when we got to the top, we slid down the hill, turning in an almost complete circle. She had no control over the vehicle. We just grabbed each other's hands held on tight not knowing if we were going to hit a tree or a ditch or turn upside down. When we finally stopped moving we were very fortunate to land off the side of the road in a relatively flat area. It was at that precise moment I knew that I didn't need to be in that profession a moment longer. My children were home facing the ice storm without me while I was risking my life on an icy road for other people's children. Please, don't misunderstand, I love all children and do wish that I could have been able to meet a need that other families may have had during that time, but it really was a time during a natural disaster that we all had to take care of our own. If we had made it there to check on them and had found some horrible situation, we don't even know what we would have been able to do for them. This was my classic problem. I never knew how much I was laying aside to help others when I needed to be helping my own.

I began to think immensely about other ways that I could help children and be able to be a part of my own children's lives. In rural Kentucky we have snow days or during that time, they were called ice days in which school is let out due to weather as busses cannot transport children to school. Michael Ray, who was a teacher, had no responsibilities at that time to his job. His only job was to be a father and caregiver of our children while I was out crusading on my own. I thought about the other ways I daily put myself in danger. I frequented active meth labs on a monthly basis. I never knew when someone might pull out a gun (law enforcement or the client). I often responded to child sex abuse reports in the middle of the night. Was this a life I wanted as a mother to Melody and Anna? Was it fair for them to see their mother's backside walking out the door to help other people's children? Sliding down the icy hill with my fellow social worker, I made a conscience decision that something needed to change.

I began to think about all the other professions out there in which I could fulfill my purpose. My purpose has and always will be child advocacy; however I was very unsure of how this could be done outside of my current position. I considered counseling and law practice; however I already had time in with the state and had begun my retirement there so it made sense in some way to stay the course. I thought about my population, my children. Most of the children were fragile in some way. Either due to abuse, neglect, mental health or educational delay, many of the foster children that I worked with were involved in some sort of special education. This was an area in which school personnel often consulted me. I was often invited for their individualized educational planning meetings. Many times I represented the therapist by reading and interpreting reports and recommendations for the best interest of the child. Since this was an area that I was already a participant in professionally, I began to research how I could serve children in education. There was an alternate certification program in which in two years I was able to get my Masters of Arts in Special Education and be a fully certified teacher. I took the necessary steps to begin the educational process and it all began to fall into place.

I was very excited. I felt surely that the Lord knew what He was doing in my life at this time. He opened so many doors for me that I barely had to wait on my own. I thought that this was the absolute best thing that could have happened to my marriage as I was on a path to the same schedule as Michael Ray. We would soon have summers off to be with our children together. We were going to get to take family trips or just lounge by the pool. There would be no more calls from law enforcement in the middle of the night to do a child welfare check. On snowy days, I would just stay home with my family. No more of that running around on ice bit. My children would see me when they got home from school. Needless to say I was very happy for the new direction my life was taking. I felt supported by Michael Ray.

I applied and was accepted into a Master's Program at Campbellsville University where I had my under grad degrees in Communications and Social Work. My educational background appears to be very eclectic as I also have a minor in theater just for kicks. I was so supported by my husband at the time that when an assistant's position in a special education classroom opened up at the local high school where he taught he encouraged me to apply for it even though it meant stepping down from my current high paying position. The benefits to the children and the family outweighed the lesser salary. I was hired in the beginning of the 2009 school year. This is the same year that I began my work on my graduate degree. So many things appeared as though they were falling in place. I was constantly thanking God for the opportunities at hand. My new job was so flexible that when my children had a program at their school, I was able to leave my classroom, zip over to their school to see them and then come back to my students.

I give you this background to bring you up to speed with the facts. When the horrible thing happened, I was in my second year of working in the special education classroom. My husband and I worked in the same building and were often able to have lunch together. My children attended elementary school on the same campus. I was in my second year of my graduate work. Everything seemed to be perfect. We had been married almost eleven years. This was a feat I never could believe happened and I was especially proud of, you see Michael Ray and I both come from broken homes and I was very stubborn that ours would be a marriage that worked. I may have even forced it to work at times, but I had a strong value that marriage was forever. I wanted to break the cycle in my family. I wanted my children to always have a mom and a dad in the same home. In fact, I was so sure that I would have been married forever, that had I had an inkling of a divorce I never would have placed children in the earth, but alas I did. I had some major blind spots on the road. My path was paved with good intentions and I have had a lot of growing up to do since the horrible thing happened.

Fast forward to now, present day. I'm telling you that the straight and narrow path can almost suffocate you at times though it is meant to put one in the right place, in the right direction, sometimes all you can do is inch forward one step at a time.

CHAPTER TWO

I currently am in my fourth year of teaching special education in my hometown, the town in which I attended high school. I have primary custody of Melody Grace and Anna Kate. We live in an adorable little town house. I have more wonderful friends than I could ever ask for. I attend a church with a solid sense of purpose that has accepted me in spite of the horrible thing. The thing that I love about God is that His plans are greater than mine. He is sovereign and I am a dumb sheep. You see, I thought that this plan that He was laying out in front of me was for my marriage, for Michael Ray and I, to be able to raise our children together, to have the same working schedule, for us to be as one. But He knew the underlying currents of this horrible thing. He knew that the horrible thing was going to happen to me and He knew that I needed a refuge. He knew that I needed to be on the same schedule as my children, not because of a man, but because He knew what I didn't, that I was going to be a single mom. I was to raise the girls on my own. They were to have weekend visitations. Life was most certainly going to change and my Creator knew that I needed this new career but not for the same reasons that I thought I needed this new career. There are so many pieces that I have seen fall into place that have helped the horrible thing become just a thing in my life. The healing that I have gone through has forever changed me.

That horrible night, the beginning of the end, started out like any other holiday weekend. Michael Ray had left to his grandmothers to help with the turkey for Thanksgiving. It was of course, Wednesday since Thanksgiving is always on a Thursday and I was enjoying the day off. I had stayed home with the children that day and was looking forward to a big weekend. You see, we had plans to go to Gatlinburg after spending Thanksgiving with his family. The cabin was already booked and I was almost finished packing the bags. My little family dream was coming to fruition. You see, the summer beforehand we had not been able to take a family vacation because I had been in summer school completing twelve hours of my Masters in June and of course, being married to a coach, he had football training and coaching which started in July. I had taken a trip with my mom and step-dad to South Carolina that July with the girls and on our way back to Kentucky we stayed a night in Gatlinburg. I remember texting Michael Ray and asking if we could take a family trip there that Thanksgiving weekend. The trip had been booked for a while and my excitement of taking the girls to the aquarium with their dad was building. The day was waning and it was about ten o'clock when the horrible thing was realized.

I had just enough ability, functioning, in my grief to call a friend to be with me. He came and brought another from church, a lady I didn't know very well, but I am grateful for them. They were calm and calculated at a time when I was not. I recall Anna-Kate, in her pajamas, looking at me, watching me fall apart. Melody had already fallen asleep in her room. She was privileged not to see what Anna saw. I do believe that Anna lost part of who she was that day. By the time my friends had left after leaving their own families to care for me, I was sitting in the recliner rocking Anna. I kept rocking and rocking. I found that rocking is a soothing movement in utter despair. It takes us back to the fetal stage where we were rocked and we find comfort in that swaying movement. I took her to my bedroom, laid her in the bed, went into the bathroom and found the Nyquil. I remember thinking that I should sleep; if I could just sleep I wouldn't think about the horrible things. I drank about one third of the bottle, laid down and slept for two hours. My mind overpowered any sleep anecdote. By then it was reaching early morning hours of Thanksgiving and I put out my smoke signals. I texted my closest four friends and said I needed them. Slowly, one by one they began to reply. My sweet friend Melissa arrived at six in the morning. I remember I had begun cleaning. I was cleaning the cracks in the hardwood floor; I sorted all of the cleaning products under the sink. I did the things you can live with for years without touching. I had to keep moving. It was a freaking holiday. The girls were still asleep as Nancy and Michelle arrived. Tammy had called because she lived out of town. They sat at dining room table. I made coffee. They sat and tried to help me piece the horrible thing together. I cleaned. Among my friends the most pressing issues were: Where would I spend Thanksgiving dinner, because obviously my plans had changed, and what was I going to do about that trip to Gatlinburg? Of course I was invited to each of their homes to spend the holiday with them. However, I knew that I could go to my mom's house which was about forty minutes away. They were insistent that I had to take the girls to Thanksgiving dinner. They were also insistent that I should still take my trip, however, I was in no condition to drive. The trip had been paid for and it was a thing that the girls were looking forward to. The trip had to happen. My beautiful friend Nancy became my first martyr. All my friends who stood beside me in the horrible thing became martyrs at some point. She sacrificed her weekend with her husband to drive my heartbroken self and my two children along with her children to Gatlinburg to stay in the cabin that I was supposed to stay in with my husband, my little family. In hind sight, it could not have been a good driving experience for her. She brought her two children along on the trip. My two children were slowly beginning to process that something had occurred that changed their course (at least for the weekend, but I'm sure they had a sense that it was forever). Poor Nancy, about every hour or so on the trip, I broke down and cried. I remember she had enough foresight to tell her children that I would be crying a lot and that they should say "I'm very sorry." to me, which they did. Nancy was so kind and compassionate to me that weekend. I know I must have gotten on her nerves. I messaged with Michael Ray back and forth the details of the horrible thing. I had so many questions and I wanted answers. I didn't often put my phone down. I think at one time Nancy threatened to throw my phone out the window. Answers, so many answers to so many questions, I needed. She knew that and she kept driving. I would cry, she would drive, I would text, and she would drive and her children would look at me and say, "I'm very sorry." Nancy is a fantastic friend. When we finally got to the cabin we brought all of our things in and assumed our rooms in the cabin. When I reached the room with the king size bed, knowing it had been intended for my husband and I, I crumbled again. Instead, Melody and Anna were my bedmates, something all three of us needed. A second nightfall was coming and I was trying to sleep again. At this point I may have been operating on five inconsistent hours of sleep over a forty-eight hour period. I dreaded the nighttime. It was the time when normal people like Nancy were tired from driving and needed rest. It was a time for children to wearily fall asleep. It was a time for me to be alone in the dark, quiet, with my own horrible anxieties and thoughts. Nancy had said that Psalms could be helpful in times of grief. As everyone in the cabin began to slumber, I went to take some more Nyquil and that gave me about three hours of uninterrupted sleep this time, but as I woke, I still had several hours with my mind which was becoming my worst enemy. It would not shut down. Now, I had that Bible app on my iPhone. Before this weekend, I really can't recall if I used this Bible app very often but as I woke I turned on my phone and began to read Psalms. I began to draw near to the Lord for comfort. I read and read and read. I made notes and saved verses in my phone for easy reference. The very first verse that began to sustain me was Psalm 143: 8 "Let the morning bring my word of your unfailing love, for I have put my trust in you. Show me the way I should go, for to you I entrust my life."

My faith has always been at the forefront of my life. That is not to say I am a perfect Christian by any means and I don't jump on any political agenda or affiliate myself with dogma but I do try to live in love of God. In the first critical hours of the horrible thing, I didn't draw near to God. I believe I was angry, not at God but just angry and in my anger I was not a seeker of God's heart. God knew this and he sent his angels around me anyway. I learned that no matter where you are, how close or how far away from God you are, He will meet you right where you are. In reference to my verse, the first verse of many that began to stick out to me, I learned to make it through the nights for the morning became my point of peace, my point of revelation that this horrible thing was not going to define me.

Throughout the rest of that weekend, in my down time, I read Psalms. It was the only thing that was able to bring me comfort. The pain that I felt that weekend was a different pain than any I had ever felt in my life. As a child growing up, I have always enjoyed trips to Gatlinburg. There is just something about the mountain air and the smell of popcorn and taffy. One of our family plans for the trip was to go to one of those old time photo booths that make the black and white pictures in the "saloon" get up and have our family picture made. It's funny because we had always wanted to have these pictures made and even in 1999 when we went to Disney World, we couldn't find a booth to have them made. I had researched online and knew that there were plenty of photo opportunities like that so it was one thing that I had looked forward to before the trip. When I was actually there with Nancy, I felt sorry for her, every time I saw one of those little shops, and they seemed to be on the corner of every block, it induced tears, because that was a symbol to me of a picture that would never be because I knew that my family as I knew it again would never be. Somehow I made it through the weekend though I don't advise travelling through Ripley's Believe it Or Not in utter despair. Some of those pictures or demonstrations would be disturbing on a good day. I did enjoy some shopping, a soak in the hot tub at the cabin and dinner out. I found a way to smile at the children as they looked at the fish in the aquarium. I had finally gotten to the point on Saturday night that I was hungry. I don't think that I had really eaten anything of substance since sometime on Wednesday before the ten o'clock hour. By the time Saturday had rolled around I was hungry. In my memory Nancy was the one who took care of the children. If I did much at all that weekend with the girls I was acting on auto pilot. The pictures from the trip appear as if I was engaged with my children so I hope that I was. Overall, I guess I am happy for the trip to have taken place. I am forever grateful for Nancy for picking up the reigns that weekend, driving us there and taking care of us all. She is to be commended for her patience because it took us an ungodly amount of time to get home on Sunday due to the holiday traffic. The children had a very rough ride on the way back to our little town.

Once we finally made it home, I had to face the inevitable: the reality of the horrible thing. The horrible thing began to have its ramifications. You see, since Michael Ray and I both worked at the same place, we both were going to see each other at our jobs. I not only had to learn how to begin my life abruptly as a single parent, I was faced daily with the reason why I was a single parent in my job. There was very little refuge from my situation.

The Monday that the girls went back to school and I went back to work is memorable. I saw Michael Ray at work in the same building with my eyes wide open to the horrible things that had occurred. Before I went to work that day, I walked my two girls into school that morning. I felt that their teachers needed to know that not everybody had a joyous holiday experience and had eaten of turkey. Knowing what I know about teachers and their relationships with students in the classroom, it is good to share when your child has gone through something traumatic and both of my children had experienced something very horrifying in just four short days. I took Anna to her kindergarten class first. I asked her teacher if I could speak to her in the hallway. I was amazed at how freely the words came out of my mouth. "Anna's father and I separated over Thanksgiving. I thought you would want to know." It was as if I were saying lines for a play. It was as if I was playing a character, until she reached out and hugged me. I fell apart. I cried on her shoulder. Of course Melody Grace was standing right beside me and I knew I needed to pull it together. I was so grateful for that teacher. I knew she cared about Anna and I knew Anna was in a safe place at school. Even now, four years later, Anna still talks about her beloved Mrs. Bray. I am grateful for teachers. I then took Melody to her classroom and asked her teacher, who had already begun the day with the students to step out into the hallway. I told her the same thing I had told Mrs. Bray as calmly as possible. She looked at me with sincerity and said "You are going to make it through this." Melody was glad to go into the classroom. For the rest of that school year, Kindergarten and third grade became my children's refuges. I am still forever grateful to their teachers for the amazing heroes they were to my girls during that time.

CHAPTER THREE

T
hings are so jumbled up in my mind as to how they occurred. I really can't recall specific order of events, but I can recall the burden that I began to live with, the burden that was extremely present and never numb. I know that in the following days I had several break downs at work. I recall locking myself in the bathroom away from the students and crying and then returning to the classroom setting. I recall trying to hold my head high while all eyes were on me. The news had become very public in just a few short days and if he and I passed in the hallway, students and staff alike would gawk and rubberneck stare. I hated that the sight of me gave them something to talk about.

There is a website that small people with small minds in small towns often access. I truly believe it the biggest source of internet bullying and ignorance I have ever seen. I refuse to promote the website and state its name however, in a matter of a week; there were over a hundred posts about the horrible thing on the website. You see on this particular website, one can hide behind a screen and post their thoughts, feelings, opinions and observations albeit true or not about a particular subject. My marriage and the fall of my marriage became that topic. At that time, I daily scrolled the internet looking for clues as to why this could be happening to me. I know now that those posts have no bearing whatsoever in my life. At the time, I didn't know where to look, who to believe. I have never wanted to crawl under a rock and hide so much in my life. My mother taught me that you didn't discuss people's problems. I was raised to be discrete in my personal life though that has always been a bit hard for me, hence this book I am writing. If any person at all can learn or grow from my transparency, then the sharing of my horrible thing has been worth it. My mother and grandmother have shown me kindness and taught me kindness to others, so when I read the following remarks online about my marital bed, you can imagine the complete chill to my spine. Never would I have had the thought to put something out on the World Wide Web as audaciously as the next comment I will share with you from that horrid website.

"I know she isn't getting it done. I know from personal experience cause I took care of it for over a year. He told me himself she wasn't doing her job in the bedroom but I have to say he makes me sick messing with children."

The amount of lies in the above statement is ludicrous. The only intent of such a statement was to hurt and cause pain. In the coming weeks there were hundreds of posts just like this one. At first I reported the threads to the webmaster stating they were libel and slander but after a while I gave up. I knew in my own heart that most, if not all, of the statements were very jumbled up and not altogether accurate or true. Granted, the choices made by Michael Ray that brought my marriage to an end were shocking but what was even more shocking was the community's response. I had to protect my children somehow, someway.

Anna-Kate had endured enough already before the Thanksgiving Holiday. You see, my precious daughter had two hospital visits and a broken arm in the month of October. She had pneumonia in one lung and as soon as it healed she had developed pneumonia again in her other lung. Perhaps the most devastating thing that had happened was that our precious babysitter, whom I had come to know, to love and adore like a grandmother, Ms. Adla Handley passed away October 27, 2010. Anna had been coming to her house every working day I had since infancy and Melody, since she was a toddler. In late November I was finally remembering to pass her street after work. I had been going there so regularly for so long that, days after her death, I still

14

had the propensity to turn the steering wheel toward her street even though I knew she wasn't there. I was beginning to remember to steer my car in the right direction after about a month of her passing. For almost five years I drove to her house every day after work. I always loved our short minute chats as I picked the girls up from her home. We talked about the weather, her grown children, her grandchildren, my children, my family, always something. She always had good advice to give and she loved my girls. Her funeral was the last time that our family, as we knew it then, was together. It was a glorious day. She was a strong, beautiful, black lady whom I loved with all my heart. None of us have ever made Anna oatmeal quite like Mrs. Adla's and Anna will still comment on our oatmeal attempts today. "Nope," she'll say, "not like Mrs. Adla's." Mrs. Adla's funeral was the kind of funeral that makes you want to leave this earth and go to heaven. My children were the only white children there, but they were asked to sit with the grandchildren. They were given a flower to put on the casket just the same. That day, I remember sitting beside my husband and thanking God that He had provided my children with such a sweet spirit of Mrs. Adla in their lives. Michael Ray was to me that day what a perfect husband needed to be. He basically held me up when grief overcame my soul. He held my hand at the gravesite and I truly felt love between us. Even though there was so much that was happening in his world that I had no knowledge of, God gave us that day to be there for each other and for our children who had endured a tremendous loss. After the funeral that day we went to visit my grandmother. There are some pictures of the three of us, Michael Ray, my grandmother and me. These were the last pictures that we had ever had made together in a marriage.

Libby Sears Blair

CHAPTER
FOUR

Since my faith is part of my identity, I have always kept a prayer journal or notes in a notebook with my Bible. If you had asked me at the time that the horrible thing happened, I would have told you that I thought I had a strong relationship with my Maker. I have always had volumes of journals but this journal was started on March 3, 2008. This is a journal I kept during that time in which I wrote simple thoughts, prayers and petitions. The very first journal entry in this journal reads:

March 4, 2008

"We don't have to earn, prove or validate who we are because everything we have has been given to us through grace not merit."

I don't always write down who said the quote or where it was read or if it my original. Sometimes, looking back, I see something I have written and I recognize growth and change in my thinking. Sometimes I just laugh and think about how silly I was about the issue I was writing about and wonder why I thought it was so pressing at the time. Most of the time, I find that it is important to review the past, process it and move forward. Through the recordings of these journal entries over time, I have a review of how the Lord has helped me work out so many things in my life. I will be sharing some journal entries with you. This is the first known journal entry that I made after the horrible thing happened:

December 4, 2010

Lord, I don't even know how to start prayers like this. I know there are times when I haven't known what to say and there are times when I haven't written anything, times when I've been distant from you and I know when those times were. I'm too busy Lord. Everyone keeps telling me to take care of myself. I haven't written in this prayer journal since my precious Mrs. Adla died. Lord, this has been such a sad season and I haven't wanted to record any prayers because I haven't wanted to speak truth about what is happening to me. You know how angry I have been and how much I am hurt. First, I want to say that I love him and I ask for healing for him. I trust that You will heal him. I ask You: What am I supposed to do while he is being healed? I just don't know. I am starting to see comfort in some things. There are so many questions still to be answered. I don't want to write a lot because I am in constant communication with You anyhow but the three things that are most on my mind at this time are:

1. *Melody Grace and Anna-Kate*

   Lord, help me answer their questions. Give them comfort and good people in their lives. Help them to see you as our guide and provision.

2. *Michael Ray*

   For Healing.

3. *Me*

   Job applications.

God, I totally respect You. You are all powerful and I am nothing without You. I am a dry and weary land in need of rain. Rain down on me sweet Jesus. Amen.

With some of the choices that Michael Ray had made, I wasn't sure of what the outcome would be. I was very concerned about how I was going to take care of my two children. In the current job that

I had, I was making approximately $900-$1000 a month. Though it had not happened yet, I felt certain that it was a matter of time before Michael Ray wasn't going to be teaching much longer.

Libby Sears Blair

CHAPTER
FIVE

When I met Michael Ray, I was a sophomore in college. We both attended the same college. I went to Campbellsville University mainly because it was where my mom wanted me to go. I didn't have a lot of say in the matter, but me being from a divorced home where I constantly felt pulled between two homes and two father figures, I was glad to go anywhere to school. My dream school at the time would have been Carson Newman in Tennessee but Campbellsville seemed to be my mother's obvious choice. This was because my mom was from Campbellsville. She had attended Campbellsville University when it was Campbellsville College and my grandmother had attended Campbellsville University when it was Russell Creek Academy, so that made me a bit of legacy, though the legacy status came from my mom and my grandmother and was never really mentioned at the College. My grandmother lived at the very far edge of campus and you basically stepped off campus, walked across the street and ended up in my grandmother's yard. At eighteen, I didn't really see what a treasure that was; however, I am so thankful now for those years that she became a special and integral part of my life. At eighteen, I felt like she was there to check up on me and feed me a good meal or two, which I didn't resent or particularly love. I think, like most eighteen year olds, I desperately wanted my freedom, but at the same time I was glad for her presence and guidance when I needed it, though I didn't see that I had either at the time.

I spent my freshman year living in the dorm going to classes, socializing, and visiting my grandmother. I didn't have a car, so many of my friendships were made by asking for a ride to the local Wal-Mart to pick up what I thought were necessities at the time such as Munchos and French Onion Dip as well as Sprite. My major was in Communications and my minor was in theater. I really thought that I had life completely figured out. Not so, but that is what I thought. I was on the President's list my first semester which surprised me greatly because I had this horrible experience with an Advanced Placement English teacher my senior year of high school who truly made me feel as if I would never amount to anything. I found out that, in college, despite her harsh grading and overly rigorous expectations, I was a good writer and reader. My freshman year of college seemed to be a success.

Toward the end of my freshman year of college, I was walking back to the dorm after being at a home basketball game. I noticed a young girl walking in the parking lot of my dorm catcalling at some of the football players that I knew. They seemed to be irritated by her and I was concerned. I guess this could be one of the first instances that I truly became a child advocate. I advanced her and asked her where her mother and father were. She said that they were several streets over. It was about nine in the evening at the time and I just asked her if I could walk her home. On the walk, I inquired as to what age she was. She said that she was ten years old. She also told me that those college boys were going to be her boyfriends. As we were walking, she saw another college student walking by and yelled out, "Hey Tammy!" and this "Tammy" came and joined us. I didn't know Tammy but I was glad to meet her, happy that I had a companion chaperoning this trip home with the child at night. In following this child, I found out we were going to have to cut through a cemetery to get to her home and so this "Tammy" and I followed her. We crossed over a major highway, through a cemetery, through a few neighborhood streets and then we made it to her house. I remember that when we got her there, her dad did not even flinch that two strangers had walked her home, in the dark, at that hour, and he just smiled, thanked us and sent us on our way. On the way back, Tammy and I had a chance to talk. As it turns out, she had known the child for some time. Our first common bond was that, she too, had been concerned for the safety of this child. Tammy was a sophomore and we knew many of same people. That night began a wonderful friendship that is still just as strong today. The little girl was used to walking around campus harassing male students and most people put up with her. I feared for her safety and general well-being and obviously I didn't think that her parents took the best care of her, so when I saw her on campus, I would take her to the meal hall with me to eat or to my dorm room to play games and I always encouraged her to head home before dark. Over time, Tammy and I had more interactions with this young child and became very close. This night began a lifelong friendship.

Libby Sears Blair

CHAPTER
SIX

During my freshman year, I had broken up with my boyfriend from my hometown. You know, he had been the boyfriend that girls have their senior year and when they go off to college, they grow apart from the boy and eventually the boy and the girl break up. This breakup was inevitable. He was a sweet guy who did nothing to deserve the break up except for the fact that I was just on a different path than he. I also had a very close guy friend from high school who became an integral part of my college life. Between him and several other relationships that were very casual, I was immersed in the world of men and really had no clue how to handle it. I think, looking back, I was never anything other than myself, which was a good thing to be.

I give you all that background just to share with you the way that Michael Ray and I had met. In the newness of the things in my life I had decided to walk onto the soccer team at my college. Now, keep in mind that one, my college was very small, and two, it was a brand new soccer team and they were just happy to have players. It was the first year of the Women's Soccer Team at Campbellsville University. I remember that they were not able to get many players to come and play because the good players were playing at other schools, so they said that they would take walk-ons. I had never even played soccer before but decided to play women's soccer at the college level. It was enticing mainly because they said that we could travel if we signed on, so I did. I didn't actually play in games, I just practiced, which was fine with me because some of those opponents were some big girls and their kicks definitely bruised my shins. If you know much about college sports, you know that the first week before classes is known as "hell week" for athletes and in my sophomore year of college, this week included me. I practiced two and three times a day, ran miles at a time and soaked myself in ice. I also noticed many of the football players that were also on campus for their "hell week". Tammy had joined me in this endeavor to play soccer, though she actually saw the field and some playing time. I think as young females we were both hyper aware of the boys on campus. Sometime throughout the week, I became aware of a party that the football team was throwing at a location called "The Shack". Of course, though we could barely move from extensive workouts, many of the girls on the soccer team got dressed up and went to "The Shack". This is the night I met Michael Ray Blair. I remember the first time he approached, he was in front of the bon fire and all I could see was his silhouette. He was big and strong looking and quite intimidating. This was late enough into the night that the girls that I was with had left and gone off with boys they had met so I had no wing girl, no one to swoop in and carry me to safety. He asked me if I had any gum and I said no and walked off. He followed me and put his hand on my shoulder which scared me a little bit. He said, "Yes, you do. You have some in your mouth." To get him to leave me alone, I took the gum out of my mouth and gave it to him and he chewed it. Later, he told me that I was so pretty that he couldn't think of anything to say to me and that was all he could think of. Of course this was after I had gotten to know him better in the daylight without any libations. We began to spend a lot of time together, as friends, since he was going through a lot of personal issues at the time and he needed a listening ear, which I was good at offering. I began to settle down with the boys and I was spending most of my time between two particular boys.

I was very drawn to my friend from high school I mentioned earlier and probably would have stopped everything if he had just said the words. One day, I was in the cafeteria after everyone was finished eating; I was drafting a letter to this young man. The letter had questions such as "We talk all of the time and get along so well, so why can't we work out?, You drive all the way here to see me and

26

I don't know if your actions speak louder than words, because you don't say how you feel." I don't know if it was a letter that I intended to give him or if it was just a cathartic release for me. I never got to consider it though because Michael Ray Blair came up to me and asked me what I was writing and I tried to explain the situation. He basically took my letter from me and boldly told me that I didn't need that letter because I had him. Being a young girl who truly wanted to be accepted, especially by a man, this was all I needed to pull me closer to him. Some of his personal issues that he was having trouble with had worked themselves out and he and I became closer and closer which widened the gap between me and this other young man. Before long, Michael Ray and I were in a boyfriend/girlfriend relationship. I enjoyed the next season of football and being a football player's girlfriend. It was like instant family. Many of the other girlfriends of players became wives and many of us are still friends today.

When the idea of marriage came up, it didn't really faze me. I was somewhat expected to marry after college and then what? I don't know. I completed my Bachelors of Arts in Communications emphasis in Electronic Media and minor in Theater. My graduation date was in April of 2000. I was married in December of 1999.

My thoughts were somewhat simple on marriage at the time. I can tell you that they have certainly evolved over time. I had this nice, big, good looking guy approach me. His words of commitment were solid. He was going to be able to make a living and he appeared to be head over heels for me. I dare say that I was tender enough that it didn't take much to swoop me off of my feet at that time. I was twenty-one years old and I was following the precepts that had been laid before me.

It seems that there was this underlying checklist I was supposed to follow: Is he smart? Yes. Is he able to provide? Yes. Can he meet your needs? Yes (well, my needs as a twenty-one year old female). Does he go to church? Yes. Are you attracted to him? Yes. All signs seemed to point to yes, so when, in October of 1999, he approached me with the idea of marriage, it was set for the end of the year.

The best thing about being married to Michael Ray was the gift of beautiful in-laws that I came to know and love. Traditionally, in-laws are the problem people in relationships, or at least that is what you read causing problems in marriages. I can truly say that was never the case for me. In fact, through the events of the horrible thing, they were some of my greatest support.

My grandmother is still my one living grandparent. Her husband passed away when I was just a toddler. My father's mother passed away when I was in college and I never met my grandfather on that side, but Michael Ray had this wonderful grandfather, his mom's dad, that we called Papaw Bob. I loved Papaw Bob. He passed away in January of 2010. I got to spend a good ten years of my life knowing and learning from this wonderful man. I love his wife, Michael Ray's grandmother, Imogene and his mother Phyllis, as well as his two aunts and uncle. One of the biggest losses in my divorce was the consistent contact I had with these wonderful people. Of course, growing up, my family had fine Christmases. My brother and I would spend time at both parents' houses for Christmas, but being shuffled between the two homes, I never quite felt at home in any place that I was, but something magical happened at Mamaw Jean's and Papaw Bob's. I felt as if I belonged, truly belonged. I didn't have to shuffle from parent to parent, not to mention how wonderful her home was, how cozy. It was like a snapshot of the Southern Living magazine at Christmas. You couldn't leave their house without receiving a hug from each person in the home. They are very loving and kind people and I am blessed that they are a part of my children's lives.

CHAPTER
SEVEN

With Christmas quickly approaching after the events of the horrible thing over Thanksgiving break, my world was being completely rocked in a huge storm that left my heart a splattered mess all over the place. Christmas had become my favorite holiday through the ten years of marriage. I also had an eleventh anniversary looming ahead. I was in the middle of the second to last trimester of my Master's work as well. I wasn't sure what the future would hold. I wasn't sure if divorce was inevitable. As a child who was the product of divorce I was very fearful of it. One of my biggest desires in life was that no matter how hard marriage became, I would stick it out because that is what I believed love was. In general, I am very raw, emotional and I don't give up easily.

During this time, my beloved friend Nancy had given me a book called <u>How to Survive the Loss of a Love</u> by Melba Colgrove, Ph.D., Harold H. Bloomfield M.D., and Peter McWilliams. She told me that it got her through a devastating break up with a fiancé years ago. I had no choice but to read it. I had to do something. There was very little that I was able to do for myself except for to pray and read. Most everything that was happening I had no control over. I had to go into my job every day. I had to go in and work in the same building with a man that, for ten years, I had shared a home, children and a bed. Now he was just this guy that I worked with walking around. It took all I had to do my job in supervision of students.

Each day that I stood in the hallway I had to see him pass by. It was an incredible amount of hurt. He had moved into a room at Mamaw Jean's and was driving back and forth to work from her home. I still loved him, I still cared about him getting to work daily and ensuring that he had his lunch and everything he needed. The reality of what was happening was not there for me yet. Nancy knew though, as did my friend Michelle. I was losing my husband. The world as I knew it was coming to an end. The ground that I walked upon was being pulled out from beneath my feet. I don't remember much that was in the book that Nancy gave me except for that it was hard to read because the title had the word Loss in it. The one thing that stuck out at me in the book was to be kind to myself. This was something I made an effort to do. Teal is my favorite color so I began to surround myself in that color. I bought shirts that were teal. I wore teal jewelry and I had some teal stationery for correspondence. My journal that I used to write in had a teal cover. There was a certain body spray I liked from Bath and Body Works so I bought it. It was called Forever Sunshine. I liked that name because I wanted Sunshine in my life. Even though I wasn't seeing it figuratively in my own life, just the name of the body spray was happy sounding, so it made me smile. I enjoy long hot baths with the water almost to the top of the tub so I took them. It was therapeutic to do nice things for myself, though it did take concentration to consider what I needed to do. In any horrible thing, I have learned that we should be kind to ourselves. This is not a time to withhold things that make us happy, however it is also not a time to overindulge and fill voids in our lives with things. It is a time to treat ourselves right and do little things that we like. It is a time to be healthy and take care of ourselves, because if we don't, no one is going to do it for us.

In the FMD (Functional Mental Disability) class that I taught, the lead teacher began a functional skill unit on knitting which was great for some of the students' dexterity. I learned how to knit during this time and found it to be a very good thing that I could do with my hands. There was a special place on my couch that I would find myself corpse like at the end of the day after I had tucked the children into bed. I usually covered up with a particular blanket that I loved at the time and either read, cried or knitted. I'm not sure how many things I knitted in the month of December 2010. It was my sad spot and I did let myself feel whatever I needed feel in that little spot of my house. My little malti-poo Rudy sat right beside me day after day, night after night. I called that spot my crying spot.

At night when I couldn't sleep and I was haunted with what was happening, I was fortunate enough to have a friend who didn't mind if I called in the middle of the night. You see, she was almost nine months pregnant with baby Ryan and she was wide-awake anyhow so she didn't care to talk to pass the time away. I am grateful for those times. Michelle, in her wisdom, knew it was over between Michael Ray and I but listened to me as I tried to hang on to something by my fingernails.

Somehow, I didn't want to believe that I was losing anything. I wanted to believe that I was worthy enough for him to come back and fix this thing, but that was not happening. Reading a book with the word Loss on the cover was acceptance and I wasn't fully able to accept the loss yet, I could feel the effects of the loss everywhere. I continued to read in Psalms. Here are my next few journal entries and the verses that seemed to get me through.

December 12, 2010

Dear Jesus,

Here are some verses that I have found hope in since I have found out about it (the horrible thing). My heart is so broken and this is the perfect way to cry out to you. I don't know what the future holds beyond the next word that I write and I am in total dependence of you.

Psalm 86:11

Teach me your way Oh Lord, that I may rely on your faithfulness; give me an undivided heart that I may fear your name.

Of course, this would be my prayer for my family:

Psalm 80:3

Restore us, O God, make your face to shine upon us that we may be saved.

God, Michael Ray and I are both looking for healing. I pray for a total reversal of how we both feel about one another right now.

Psalm 88: 13

But I cry to you for help, Lord. My morning prayer comes before you.

Broken Dreams

Lord, You know that I have always wanted You in my life and now all that has fallen apart. My heart breaks in a whole new way every day. I will continue to put my trust in You. I really don't know what to ask about the future. I know I love that man that You gave me. I know I want him to be all that you created him to be. I know that is his choice and all I can do is lean on you and depend on you and make decisions for myself right now. Thank You for the friends that You have put in my life and for people who love me and pray for me and care for me.

I do ask for Michael Ray's total healing, for him to be whole. Lord, that he would overcome the trauma that he has faced in this world and that it would not be a crutch to him as he is a husband or a parent or a teacher. Thank you for Your deliverance in him keeping his job and our means of income for now even though we really don't have anything right now.

. Please guide my steps in my next career move. If I could work in the county that I live in that would be what I want more than anything. Help me to work on forgiveness where I need to. Help me to know what I need to know. Help me to see what I need to see. Help, help, help.

Amen, Libby

Not all of what I am sharing do I remember very well. In fact, I might tell you that I didn't feel the way that you are seeing and reading, however I must have because it is recorded that way. I do however; remember how clearly I felt on this particular day.

Our family was accustomed to going to church weekly on Wednesday nights and this continued for a while. In fact, I was working in the nursery at the church that we attended with a preschool group. Michael Ray was used to working and spending time with the youth group, with the students that he spent the day with at the high school. There was a particular night during this time that I couldn't function in the preschool setting and I thought that the praise and worship music might be soothing to my soul. I won't ever forget a lady in the church who hugged me. It was the first hug that I truly felt completely embraced and cared for. It was tight and I needed that. I remember that during the silent time for meditation and prayer, I somehow made my way to the altar, just to pray and cry. Everywhere I went I cried, but my purpose was to pray. My eyes were closed and I was uttering words from the depths of my heart. I began to feel many people around me. I didn't look up, but there were people touching me and praying for me and then I realized that Michael Ray was near me and there were people in the room praying for him too. Eventually the music faded and I got myself up and I was able to make my way back to my seat where my friend Melissa sat. That night, Michael Ray came to the house to tell the girls goodnight and remember that he picked me up and carried me to bed and tucked me in, just the same as he did the girls. I was emotionally drained and he saw the toll it was taking on me. I was no fool to believe that this one action fixed everything and I think that I was so depleted that I wasn't even hopeful. I think he was doing what any human would do for another human in my state. I was beginning to sleep through the night due to exhaustion.

In education, one of the most glorious things you can hear from time to time is these two words-"snow day". Another day captured in my memory is the much needed "snow day" I remember getting the call and of course the first thing I did was call Michael Ray at Mamaw's house to let him know he didn't have to come to work that day. Now many women in my shoes would have delighted to purposely not call him and have him drive all the way to work only to find out that there was no school that day, but consideration for others is in my core.

I had tried to get into see a therapist several times at this point but there was such a wait time that it was very difficult to get in. I knew since there was snow on the ground there might be some cancellations so I began to call Dr. Urey's office. Dr. Urey happened to be a therapist that I had worked with professionally several times and I had come to admire his work with patients, so now that I needed someone, he was my obvious choice. I was able to get in that day and see him. From that day forward, he became an integral part of my journey.

This is the journal entry from that day:

December 13, 2010

Dear God,

It is five days until my eleventh anniversary. He has hurt me so much and all I want to do is be with him. How can someone have two emotions like that at the same time? He has said some very hurtful things that I lay at your feet. I don't know what to do with them. I said mean things too. I'm not sure what to do when he says he needs space. He has shared his entire life with me for eleven years and now it is all taken away. Lord, I know You are a God of grace, mercy and justice and You hold all the cards in Your hand. I can only plead to you what I want and you can grant it. Am I even right to ask you for total renewal, restoration and blessings on this family?

It's a snow day today God. I changed my whole career path and everything so I could be home with my partner on a day like this and it is all missing.

I'm going to try to get into Dr. Urey today. I don't think that he is the answer to all of my questions, but hopefully he can provide some clarity because right now I am just a big mess. I'm hurt and confused, God. The Enemy has done a great job on this one and he is basking in mine and my children's pain.

I lift my eyes up to the hills, where does my help come from? My help comes from the Lord, the maker of heaven and earth. Psalm 122 (I think).

He said he thinks I'll be mad at him for the next 20 years. Lord, if your goal for us is repair, help me to forgive and learn how to live past the pain. I want that for me, him and the children.

***I didn't realize at the time that I could pray this last statement and repair could occur in other ways than reconciliation. ***

Lord, give me strength today. Days like this are the worst because these are the days I miss him the most. Help me meet my children's needs and be kind to them. They deserve that from me as much as possible. I want help God, please.

Love, Libby

The meeting with Dr. Urey was impeccable timing. I had very rapid speech in the one-hour session. I tried to get as much out as I could. It was basically a meeting that began the year and half long therapy work that I needed to get through this crazy situation in my life. He was very good at gently expressing to me what everyone else seemed to already - This was the end.

Days away from my eleventh anniversary and Christmas, we had to decide what to do about the commemorative dates. I suggested that we take the day of our anniversary to Christmas shop for the children and at least spend the day together. I asked that he keep his phone put up out of respect for me. I recall that we spent most of the day walking around the mall buying gifts for Melody and Anna. I recall him taking long bathroom breaks where I believe he was either on the phone or texting. He and I were civil but not happy. It was really kind of a miserable day. I think on this day I may have had a glimpse of what everyone else already knew and saw. Here is my journal entry for the beginning of that day:

December 18, 2010

Lord,

You know what today is and how I feel. You know I need a good day of peace and love. Help me to show only love and kindness today. I don't know what the future holds but you do. Give me time to take care of gifting my children and nurturing them today. Give me the right words to say to my husband. Help me sort through things in my mind. Lord, be with my precious babies at their grandmother's. Have their family show love and support to them. Speak to me and through me, God. Amen!

At some point during the Christmas Season, he had come over to the house and helped me decorate. I had a lot of commemorative ornaments from "Our First Christmas" to "Our New House", "Baby's First Christmas" etc. I didn't want to see them and be reminded of the better days that I was not currently experiencing. He was thoughtful enough to put those up for me. The house was decorated as much as I could stand for this was a very sad Christmas and it was finally Christmas Break. I could finally get out of that school where the pain occurred every day. I could finally leave the town where the crazy citizens had made it their business to write all about my personal life on a ridiculous web site. I packed the girls up and we drove to Louisville. I was so glad to be at my best friend Tammy's house. She opened her home to me and it was a place I could truly be me and let my guard down. I was able to talk to her about all of it. Tammy had just become a single mother of four in the year prior to my situation. I remember as soon as I had walked into her house, her youngest Aslan was walking down the steps. I had not visited in awhile and she said, "My daddy doesn't live here anymore." I remember thinking how sad it was to hear those words and that my children would possibly also say those words in the near future to others. Tammy knew my journey and she knew it would be hard. Some of her best advice was that either way would be hard, to stay together and work it out or to divorce and that there was no shame in either path I took. I remember how exhausted I was at her house in this week before Christmas. She suggested that we all pack up for the afternoon and go to the Y to work out and to swim. I remember at first, we dropped the kids off at the childcare center and then she and I did some elliptical work. Exercise had not been a part of my routine prior to this trial so I was very out of shape and unhealthy. One thing about Tammy is that, though she is fabulously physically fit, she always slows her pace down for me so that I get the benefit of the workout. Maybe someday, I will slow my pace down for her now that I am a runner as well! After the cardio, we went to the bar to stretch when she finally began asking me the questions that needed to be asked. I remember telling her about my response to his actions and his response to my actions. I will never forget her saying to me- "Libby- it just doesn't sound good." I had been hearing those words from my girlfriends in Hodgenville but I needed to hear them from someone who wasn't IN the situation, from someone who had known me longer. I was beginning to get it. The acceptance was starting to come through, days before Christmas. **My marriage was over.**

After our workout we got the kiddos and took them to the indoor pool. They swam and enjoyed themselves. They got to be children with other children. They needed this time and so did I. I recall looking up at the windows from the pool and I could see the snowflakes falling while I was in the water.

This was my prayer that night:

December 21, 2010

Lord, thank You for a safe place to be right now. Thank You for encouraging me to seek You daily. I will. I want to. I'm really sad right now. I have no questions answered and I don't know how You are going to answer them. I just know to fully depend on You. I can feel him pulling away. I know he is Yours. Give me strength, patience and kindness. Help me help my daughters through this time. Give me words and actions to say and do. Peace, healing and strength in this very house that I am in right now.

Amen, Libby

We left the day before Christmas Eve and came back to our home. My safety net I had in Tammy was gone and I was back in uncharted waters. I didn't know how we were going to do Christmas together or apart. I was so weak that I wasn't able to give it a lot of forethought. I thought my girls needed to be with their father.

CHAPTER EIGHT

An interesting thing happened on Christmas Eve, my cousin, Laura, (she is my grandmother's brother's daughter, which makes her a second cousin, right?) called me to tell me that she had some things that she wanted to drop off on her road trip to visit her family for Christmas. She has some glasses that had belonged to my great-grandmother as well as my great grandmother's wedding set. I was kind of happy about this. It is nice to be given family heirlooms regardless and ever nicer to have a sense of traditionalism and some articles that have stood the test of time. This was a time in my life I was craving consistency. I valued these things when she brought them. I even decided to wear my great-grandmother's diamond ring on my wedding ring finger. I had been wearing nothing since the night before Thanksgiving when the horrible thing happened and I had taken my rings off and set them on the kitchen window shelf. They remained there even at the moment that I was putting on another ring. I have to admit it did feel good to put that ring on my finger after going a month without wearing anything. It was a very strange feeling to go for a month without wearing anything as for almost eleven years; I had faithfully and happily worn a wedding band. I was grateful to be able to show that I was a married woman; however I was also grateful that it wasn't the wedding set that was the unity of my marriage. I was still legally married and it was important for me at that time to show that and my cousin brought me just the gift that I needed for that purpose. It was a sweet, dainty ring that was certainly used for a different purpose than it was originally intended. I have had friends in my similar situation call this type of ring the "Leave Me the Hell Alone" ring. It is a type of ring that is worn on the wedding ring finger of the separated or divorcing woman so that they are not approached by other men during their time of pain and chaos because all that does is add to the drama.

I was happy to have this ring given to me by a sweet cousin. Her intention was to pass on a few family heirlooms. Little did she know it would become so much more to me.

As it turned out, on Christmas Eve, I drove the girls to my mom and stepdad's house and we celebrated there. The plan was that Michael Ray would stay Christmas Eve night at our home on the couch so he would be there when the girls opened their presents from Santa and then all of us would go to his Mamaw's house which I was glad to do because I love that family so much. I decided to forgo seeing my father that year as it was all too much. I saw him in the days after Christmas. I just didn't want to have to explain everything to him on Christmas. After Christmas Eve Dinner and gift exchange at my mom's, the girls and I trekked out of her house only to drive home in three or four inches of snow. I was bound and determined that I would get to my house for the girls to open their gifts from Santa in the morning with their dad there. After a very long, icy drive, we made it home safely and he was there to help me carry sleeping girls into their bedrooms.

This was the prayer at the start of the day on Christmas Eve 2010. Most of my prayers are written in the morning so that I can focus on Light and warmth.

December 24, 2010

Happy birthday Jesus. You are all I can joyfully focus on this Christmas. Thank You for Your message of peace, hope, joy and ultimate sacrifice. I need you in my life more than ever. I'm in pain and Your story helps. —Your life on earth and your promises of a kingdom in heaven. You, as conqueror of all, make that pain easier to bear. I ask for help in healing my pain. I ask for help healing his pain. Lord, carry my children when I can't. Keep them protected.

Please be with us these next two celebration days. Guide me in what to say and do. Give me peace and contentment in You. Help! Amen.

I remember going into my bedroom, shutting the door and waiting for Christmas morning, not in anticipation but in dread. Finally the morning had begun with two excited little girls opening their presents from Santa. I was glad to give them this time together with their family. Soon after presents had been opened and breakfast dishes had been cleaned it was time to go to Mamaw's house. All four of us got in the car and drove the snowy, somewhat icy roads to her home where, no matter how sad you were; your spirits could be lifted for a moment. However, it was too much for me to take in all at once. It was teasing, knowing that this was a beautiful part of my life that I may not get to experience anymore. Though my heart wanted to love and be with those around me, the aunts, the uncles, the cousins and especially Mamaw, I just wept. I found a place in the house next to the washer and dryer to myself and silently cried, then I would get myself together and go out to see the family again which would lead me back to tears. I loved them all so very much. I'm not sure how much of the current situation Mamaw was aware of, but at some point in the day she found me and took me to the laundry area in her house and said something like this to me. "No matter what happens between you and Michael Ray, I will always love you and you are always welcome here in my home." That was the most comforting thing that I had felt that day. That was Christmas 2010. That was all I could handle. Before long the day was over. Michael Ray drove us back home and the girls and I stayed and he left.

I used the rest of the time that break to focus on my master's work and try to wrap my head around the changes that I had to make in my life. When everything began to happen in November, I knew that I was not going to be able to spit out papers on research based literacy strategies. I had two professors at that time. I just sent them an email that simply stated that I was having some major changes in my life and that I would not be able to work on anything for at least a month. I shared that information with another gal in my cohort and everyone seemed to truly understand. They seemed to really care that I was struggling. Both of my professors emailed me to get my work to them when I could. I used that break to get back on track and finish those two courses.

CHAPTER
NINE

New Years of 2011 was very strange for me also. This of course was the first New Year's in twelve years that Michael Ray and I had not spent together. Of course, we were only separated at this time and he still owned the house with me, so if he came over or wanted to sleep on the couch, I tried to oblige though it was very painful to know your heart was laying on the couch and not in the room with you where it had always been. He still held my heart at this point. If you knew all of the circumstances, you would say that there is no way that he could have still held my heart at this point but I guess I had a seriously strong love for him and I still was okay with him being around. Perhaps I had some hope that he would find me worthy of making amends and then our children wouldn't go through a divorce. In my deepest heart of hearts, I knew he was slipping away. Still, I let him stay on the couch that night. I remember that the girls had gone to his mother's house and I stayed home by myself that night.

He and I had tried to have several conversations over the course of the break and none of them gave any resolution to any problem that we faced. The next day off that we both had was January 17, 2011, which was Martin Luther King Jr.'s birthday. We had resolved to table everything until then. This gave us seventeen days to consider our lives together and to gain some ground. I went to bed around ten that evening and scribbled this last entry in my journal before I went to sleep. I knew at some point he would come in during the night and sleep on the couch.

December 31, 2010

I am still sad. I am still in pain. I don't want him to go, but I don't want to feel like this when he is here. He can barely look at me. We have resolved not to talk about anything until January 17th. That's the first day we are out of school and we will have to be together and talk then.

Lord, fill up my empty places so that I can experience Your unfailing love each morning, that way when people show me love, it overflows. I can feel You right now Dear Jesus. Amen.

I read in a book by Angela Thomas called <u>Wallflowers Don't Dance</u>, over the summer of 2010 about her sadness after her divorce. She wrote about sleeping and waking up and not knowing what to do next. I couldn't really identify with what she had written at the time but in these early months of 2011, I began to understand. The sadness was overwhelming and I would try to follow her advice in her book, which I will now paraphrase for you (atrociously): "If you don't know what to do next, just do something. If the counter needs to be wiped, just wipe the counter." I know it sounds like such simple advice but it was something that I needed to learn to do. I am super guilty of looking at big pictures and not breaking down things to manageable tasks. This advice was incredible for me. It truly had me getting things completed. It was often what made me complete the laundry and get dinner on the table.

A couple of years prior the this horrible thing happening in my life, I had been part of a Women's Ministry Team at my church and we had taken a trip to see Lisa Whelchel, whom you know as Blair from The Facts of Life. Remember The Facts of Life? Tutti, Jo, Natalie, Blair and Mrs. Garrett? I always thought it was weird that Mrs. Garrett was on that show and Different Strokes. Wow, that identifies me as an eighties kid for sure, but anyway, we took a trip to Bowling Green, Kentucky to hear Lisa Whelchel who is now a Christian Author and Speaker. I truly enjoyed her ability to speak with very few notes, be entertaining and get her point across. She speaks to large crowds as if you are sitting next to her at a table in a quaint little restaurant. One of her main points of her talk was parenting and I am always up for some parenting advice, that's for sure. My friend Nancy truly had to remind me of one piece of advice that Lisa Whelchel had when the sadness would overwhelm me in such a way that I couldn't fix dinner and then the guilt would set in of not being supermom to my children. Nancy would say, "Remember, Lisa Whelchel says it's okay if your kids eat cereal for dinner every once in awhile." Nancy would remind me that I was a good mom and that my kids were lucky to have me. Ironically enough, I had to Google Blair's real life name to make sure that I wrote it correctly for the purpose of this book and I saw that Lisa Whelchel has also endured a divorce situation in 2012. Funny how her inadvertent advice got me through a rough night or two. It is also comforting to know that no one is immune from troubles in this life.

Another thing that happened during these winter months was that my friend Michelle, the one who could always take a call in the middle of the night because she was up with pregnancy, had her baby. There was something very comforting about holding her baby. I nicknamed him my Baby-Love. Since she had five children already, she was very willing to let others hold Baby Ryan as often as we wanted. Baby Ryan offered me an incredible amount of warmth, peace and innocence that I needed to have in my heart during that time.

.

CHAPTER
TEN

I was very apprehensive about seeing Michael Ray at school again when we started back after Christmas Break. That Sunday night before the week began, I wrote the following journal entry:

January 2, 2011

2 Corinthians 4:16-18, The Message

"So we're not giving up, how could we? Even though on the outside, it often looks like things are falling apart on us, on the inside, where God is making new life, not a day goes by without his <u>unfolding grace</u>. These hard times are small potatoes compared to the good times, the lavish celebration prepared for us. There's more here than meets the eye. The things we know are here today, gone tomorrow, but the things we can't see now will last forever."

Lord Jesus, I'm so sad today. I know that I know all of Your promises, but I'm having a hard time holding on to those promises. I am dreading painful decisions that lie ahead. All I want is my family together but that means Michael Ray has to have many things different in his own heart and life. I just pray over him and lift him up to You. I lift our marriage up to You. Be with us this next week as we are at our jobs. Lord, help me to focus on each task at hand so that I am not lost without You.

Thank You for all of the good in my life: my two beautiful girls, my family and friends, my home, my car, my warmth, my meals and my bed. Thank You that I have had this time off for reflection and rest. You know I have needed it. Thank You for your promises that I am trying to cling to. May they be more real to me now than ever before.

Amen, Libby

When school started back, in January, in the cold, I remember that it felt much that way in my own life, somewhat bleak, cold and dark. Each day seemed to be the same. Day in and day out, I forced myself to get up and take care of the girls, to get them dressed, fed and to school. I faced going to work each day, seeing my husband at his job. There were times when we tried pleasantries to one another and then there were times when we basically passed and ignored each other, probably because we didn't know what to say to each other. How do you sum up- "Hi, I'm sorry this horrible thing has happened and your life is changing"? Neither of us really knew what to say in passing and I am firm believer that if you can't say anything nice, you should say nothing at all. The girls did okay. I was in such a fog with my own feelings that I can't honestly say how they felt all the time. Looking back, I think Melody was my stoic protector and held so many things in. Anna, however, showed her emotions more outwardly. She talked about how she felt, she drew pictures and she, like me, cried. She must have internalized her sadness in the form of a stomachache which she complained about quite often. My mom and my step dad stopped in every few days to check on us, and my dad called me quite often just to see how I was doing. I couldn't really answer questions. My world was slipping through my fingers.

January 12, 2011

Here I am Lord, it's a snow day. It's time that I have chosen to spend with You in depth. Lord, thank You for the protection you have placed around me. Thank You that I have been able to do school work and have been able to stay calm.

Lord, help me to be a strong mother to my children. Help me to have joy in being their mother. I just ask that they go untouched by pain during this time. I pray for Anna's little stomach pains. Please keep her well.

Jesus, I don't know what the future holds and I don't want to ask for anything not in Your will. I will just continue to lay this situation at Your feet and ask for comfort and provision during this time.

Lord, touch Michael Ray in such a way that that he cannot deny your love and truth. Give him that nudge to reach out to people who are reaching out to him. I thank You most for Your protection You are giving me to daily get up and take care of my babies.

Lord, I lay our finances and our home in Your hands. I ask that overall You direct me where You want me in a job and if I am to live in this home. If Michael Ray comes here today, I ask that You help me be strong.

Lord, I believe in You and your unfailing love to fill me up in places that have been punctured. I love You Jesus.

Amen

In my mind, there was a big build up to January 17, Martin Luther King Day, and I was so hopeful that he would say that he wanted to work things out, that he wanted to get back together, that the horrible thing could be fixed. That day, we planned for him to come over. It was regular for him to come over because he would come to see the girls and take them to McDonald's or something like that. They were always so happy to see their daddy. I had seen my therapist, Dr. Urey that day and was talking over the planned "meeting". At that time my heart was still hopeful that we would somehow work out. Dr. Urey said that if I wanted him to move back in, I should ask him to. He would have two choices, to say yes, or to say no. I tried to sit down and talk with him and he did not have anything to do with that. He mainly tried to talk to the girls. As he was walking out the door, I finally asked him if he would move back, to try. He said he didn't think that he could do that. I think I was stunned and shocked but numb at the same time. I think, deep in my heart, somewhere I knew that he would say no. I just stood there with the happenings becoming clearer to me than they were before. I was recognizing the power of the word NO.

Libby Sears Blair

CHAPTER
ELEVEN

My journaling kept me going. It was a place to sort out my thoughts. Much of what I was going through was a fog. Somehow I got through Valentine's Day that year, not that I think Valentine's Day is a very big deal. I find it to be somewhat superficial and I am much more appreciative of a man who doesn't need a holiday to prompt his feelings, however I guess I did like the holiday in the past. Anytime there is a time to celebrate love, I think that is important. Baskin Robbins had an ice cream out that month listed as a flavor of the month. It was called Heartbreak Healer. It had candy hearts and dark chocolate chunks in milk chocolate mousse ice cream. While it didn't exactly heal a broken heart, I do think ice cream is soothing to the soul and it tasted really good!

February 12, 2011

It has been a very long time. Hard to believe that I haven't written in a month. Fearful to write what is happening in my life because then it becomes real and he is not here. But it is real and he really is not here. He says that he wants a divorce; that he doesn't want to try. At the same time, I have completed my entire Master's Program except for my PRAXIS exams, which I take one month from today. The Lord has been talking to me. Daily, He reveals truth to me in various forms about where I am and where I need to be and what I should be seeing. He never lets go and he lifts me up as His daughter.

He has provided me with people in my house to love me, to care about me and to talk to me. He has given me strength to be a mom when it is hard. He has given me strength to work and see Michael Ray each day at school. He gives me strength to check on Michael Ray and care for Michael Ray.

Lord,

Thank You for your provision. Thank You that I see that there is life outside of Michael Ray Blair. Thank you that I am ultimately Yours and that You take care of me and that You meet my needs and that my growing pains actually grow me up to You. I only want what You want.

I ask for Your guidance...continued guidance and direction. Clarity and truth, please God.

Amen

On February 23rd, I sat in a ladies group at church where they were doing a study on an abundant life. I wasn't really into being a joiner at this point, but I think someone invited me and there I sat wounded and feeling different than all of those other women who were married and had a right to be there. (At least that is how I felt at the time).

Can you imagine how that must have felt to think about an abundant life, knowing what I was going through? I know people had to know what was going on in my life, that people were talking about it, that it was a part of gossip circles, but I didn't dare open up or share personal details with anyone unless they were in my circle. At one point I tried making a list to see who all knew what I was going through. I wrote down everyone that I could think of that I had personally spoken with about my situation, including my family and there were no more than fifteen people on the list. When I felt like everyone was talking about me, it was important to know who was on my side. I sat silently in a room with ten or so women and just listened to the study. Their concerns in their lives seemed so arbitrary, so normal compared to the storm I couldn't get out of, yet I sat silently and listened. I jotted notes down about points of the study that spoke to me. One thing that I found important was that no matter my situation or others in the room, God can speak to you right where you are.

John 10:10

The enemy has come to kill, steal, and destroy but I have come so that you might have life and have it abundantly.

The Enemy was suffocating me at this point in my life. Some of the quotes I jotted down as a result of the abundant life study were:

"The abundant life is when, in the midst of your <u>impossible</u> situation, you say, 'Now is the time!'"

"One of the most fantastic attributes of God is simply that He can."

"God is predictable in character but unpredictable in His activity. " (Didn't I know that?)

The author of the study was Priscilla Shirer. I had read her book, _Discerning the Voice of God_ before and I knew that I liked her words and that they were the real deal. The thing that stuck out at me the most in this (and I have shared it with many people since): You can pray to God and ask for exactly what you want, after all He is the one who puts the desires in your heart when He created you, but you can and should also say- Please, do that which I am asking **or something better!** I love the something better part. We don't ask God to do things that we don't want, but oftentimes, His plan is so much better than anything we could ever fathom. I have pondered this particular thought many times in which the horrible thing became just a thing.

This moment is pivotal in my story. I was standing in the kitchen looking over the counter at Michael Ray in the dining room where he sat down at the dining room table. He looked at me and said the words I needed to hear, the words that helped me let go. He said, "I want a divorce." As I heard those words for the first time, they angered me. It might have been the first time that I had gotten past sad to an angered state. I said, "Okay." Just as simple as that. I was thinking... You want a divorce? Fine, you get a divorce. You want to throw away a good wife and children? Okay, do it. I took off my great-grandmother's ring off of my wedding finger and slipped it to my right hand. It was the best symbol I could think of during the horrible thing to show any type of strength. I looked at him and said, "I will be okay. I will get through this, but you never will." I honestly think those were the meanest words that I could have possibly said because I said them in anger. I'm sure I said other things that were angry and mean and hurtful along the way, but those were the meanest words I recall saying directly to him. I was mad that anyone would choose not to be a part of US. In my mind, he was giving up. The horrible thing was becoming the most horrible thing I could imagine enduring.

The following Saturday I was working at a National Forensics League Tournament at the school. I was the middle school speech coach, so at this tournament, I just helped out where I was needed. As it turned out, I was needed in the hospitality room more than anywhere else, which was good for me because I was slated to take my PRAXIS test very soon. So between changing out the tea and coffee and replacing breakfast casseroles with soups and such for lunch, I had time to sit and go over my notes for the test.

I always enjoyed my time with the people that were involved with speech through LaRue County Forensics, however on this day, I was content to stay to myself and be the quiet servant type. Being a part of such a small town, one of my middle school student's mother was married to one of the coaches with whom Michael Ray coached. She had become my friend through various football games as well as speech tournaments that I had taken her daughter to compete. Just months earlier she and her husband had invited us over to swim in their pool after a particularly hot evening scrimmage in the late summer. Looking back, that was just one of those nice nights that I had felt that all was right with the world. Maybe it was that Jennifer and I were becoming good friends, maybe it was because I was glad that I had a fellow coach's wife as a friend, maybe it was the wine that came out almost steamy as it hit the glass that evening or maybe it was the shooting stars I recall overhead as we floated in the pool, but as much as I had enjoyed our friend's company that night I had enjoyed Michael Ray's. That man without a shirt on was a man that I was always proud to call mine.

My, how the tables had turned. I was thankful that as soon as Jennifer had heard about the horrible thing, she remained my friend.

She reached out to me as not many people did or knew how to do which I fiercely appreciated. So many people didn't know what to say, so they said nothing. This was not a time to act normal or say nothing. This was a time to at least acknowledge that a family was torn and that people were hurting rather than gossip behind someone's back and then just smile as they walked by. Jennifer never did that. She knew I was hurting and she reached out, let me cry and listened. I learned a lesson through this time. Even if I don't know what to say in someone's sad time, I will acknowledge them. There won't be a time where I will pretend I don't know someone is hurting. My friend Claire and I discussed this and she said that when her father died and she felt like the whole world was passing by and going on without her, the people that stopped and acknowledged her pain meant the most. She said that looking back at her horrible thing, those are the people that she remembered. You don't have to know what to say and you don't have to ask any questions but it is right to say, "I'm sorry, I know this must be hard." Or "I've been thinking about you." Jennifer was one of those people for me.

She came into the hospitality room that afternoon and noticed my ring was on my other finger. She was one of the first people that I had told that I was officially getting divorced. She didn't seem shocked by it. In fact, I think most people weren't.

Chapter Twelve

It was in the following days that more decisions were made. I/We needed to find an attorney. We settled upon a man who had been a Sunday School teacher for us and was a friend of mine through work. I believe that he had been someone who was rooting for us, who was pulling for us and it actually saddened him to think that he was going to assist ending the marriage, but at the same time, I think he knew that it was healthier for us to be apart. As I faced the fact that I was getting divorced, as I faced the fact that my forever was ending, I began to think logistically. Did I want to continue staying in the house? I needed to pass the PRAXIS for special education. I needed to ace that thing so I could begin to take care of myself and be employed. I began to think about child support amounts. I considered what a divorce looked like. There is a petitioner and a respondent. I recall a conversation with Michael Ray in which I stated that, since he wanted the divorce, he should be the petitioner. I didn't want that for me. I didn't want to be on record as the one who wanted everything over. He agreed to be the one. I don't know if he had any strong thoughts or feelings about it but I did. I really don't know where his thoughts were during this time. I know that he has his own story about the terrible thing and that it is different than mine and I am sure that he has his own experiences and lessons from his story. The division was becoming evident and clear. It is possible that the division was actually there all along, and had been ignored, covered up and concealed for lack of knowing how to handle it. Now, it was blazing down the center of US like a hot blue flame.

When we met with our attorney, the language of divorce became clear as well. They use words like child support, division of assets, tax exemptions, no fault. I became accustomed to the words much quicker than Michael Ray did, because I had this job where I saw these words applied in other cases. I was a little indignant that now the case was mine. My children now had a case number through child support. That was frustrating to me. Our attorney commended us for handling the situation so well. I remember how calm I was in the meeting, facing facts, trying to decide what would benefit Melody and Anna best as well as me. I had to remind myself repeatedly that I had to start thinking about me first and not him. I was going to be living life as head of the household with two children. I was going to be the words I hated to think of myself as: SINGLE MOTHER.

The words- "Single Mother" made me angry. They made me feel as if I were not whole. My friend, Tammy, while she was going through her divorce, said to me several times, "I don't want to be the poster child for single mothers." I always thought of a milk carton with the missing children on it, and had this crazy image of this broken, sad mother trying to hold it together with her children in the same picture. In the very deep, back of my mind, I knew that wasn't us. I knew that we were better than that, she and I. I knew that we would rise again. Those thoughts were very much suppressed but they did exist.

In meeting with an attorney, in facing facts, I focused on the day-by-day happenings but began, also to focus on just a little bit more. Michael Ray and I began to establish a routine for visitation with the girls and the Saturday that I was to take my PRAXIS was quickly approaching. I was so nervous. I knew so much was riding on this test. I knew that if I flopped, I would have to go back to social work. I was banking on becoming a teacher and being a single mom. It was going to be the way I supported myself. Now, I have said before that God has all things taken care of and in our fog, we fail to realize it and this was one of those times.

As I sat to take the test, I began to answer each question with positivity that I was correct in my answers and with each question,

I became more and more confident that there was a future! It was becoming tangible.

Libby Sears Blair

CHAPTER
THIRTEEN

Spring Break was quickly approaching and we had decided that the girls would be with me over the break. I can't recall exactly why we had decided that. Much like Christmas, I packed the girls up and I headed to Tammy's, my safe haven. I needed time to process things and talk things over with her. I love her home, her style and the fact that she just gets me. The girls love going to her house so they can spend time with her children and that gave me a break from the constant care that they needed from me. Spring Break at Tammy's was a healthy time for me where I was able to talk about what was going on, how my heart was hurting and healing at the same time. It was a time where I ate healthy and I exercised and took care of myself. Tammy encouraged long hot baths (though single moms rarely have time for such luxuries), a glass of wine and reading a magazine. There were days that I babysat her children as well as my own while she worked and then we all had a dinner plan for the evening. It was during this trip that I began to consider moving back to the Louisville area. I had always wanted to move back to Shelbyville, the town which I consider my home, though I had no job opportunities to be able to do so at that time, but the thought was beginning to merge in my mind. A close second would have been living in the Louisville area. I began to explore and fall in love with Louisville.

My mom has always talked about Louisville with a feeling of

distaste. When I was younger, Louisville was an industrial town. While I was gone through college and young adult years, Louisville really developed itself and became a very fun and beautiful area with odd nooks and crannies that I was learning to enjoy. My children were discovering unique things to do there as well. We took a day and enjoyed the Waterfront Park with the girls and Caedmon, Tammy's son. We walked all over parts of the Louisville loop and visited the Abraham Lincoln Statue. While this adventure is not really all that spectacular, it is an adventure I am happy to say was beginning to replace other happier times when my family was an US. I was beginning to see that I could provide fun opportunities for my children alone.

Another fun time that we enjoyed on this trip was the night when we went to a pizza place in Southern Indiana that Tammy knew about. I recall two things about that evening. One was the sweet little miniature train that ran around the building and delivered things to your table. My children loved that. They thought it was so much fun. Tammy was showing that I didn't have to have a husband with me to do family things with my girls. The other thing that Tammy showed me, whether she realized it or not, was how she was moving on in another way. While we were eating she received a text message from a man that she really thought a lot of and had recently begun dating. I remember her face lighting up as she read the text. I remember coaxing her to read it aloud which she was both happy and embarrassed to do. She then asked, after reading it, "What should I write back?" It showed me a spark of the future again. There was a possibility of partnership again someday! We both thought of the many ways to respond and of course she made up her own reply and sent it. Only later would I understand the magnitude in hitting "send" on something as simple and as seemingly arbitrary as a text message. On all levels, my friendship with her served me well. She was HOPE!

One day during that visit, I received a phone call from Michael Ray. He said he wanted to talk. He said he had figured out where he was going to get an apartment. Wow! Plans were in works for him to officially have a place of his own and move out of his mamaw's. At this time, it was quite shocking to me, concerning to me that he thought he could just begin using our money and move our things into some "affordable" old apartment. Once again, I thought about him throwing it all away-casting your pearls before swine, if you would. He didn't seem to care or see it the way I did, not that I brought up my feelings to him anymore. I began to realize it is futile to discuss your feelings with someone who is not all in; someone who doesn't care to live with you doesn't care to hear your feelings so I listened to what he wanted to do. I rationally responded that it was good. What else could be said? The blue blaze between us was still burning bright. I was further away in actual distance and he was further away in a relative way. We were both moving away. It was happening, I couldn't stop it and I was facing it.

During this time, I had a very unsettling dream. I dreamed that I was back in the Roman Coliseum at the time when they flooded the bottom of it to have battleship wars. There was a great crowd of people in the stands and the girls and I were standing together on an island of rock (what would be considered upstage right, for my theatre people). We were not in the show and there really wasn't anything happening at the time. It was as if the show was going to begin in about fifteen minutes and everyone was filling the stands. I looked out into the stands and I saw what I knew to be five different hit men circling the crowd. I don't know how I knew that is what they were but I knew (it was dream world). I watched in fear from the rock position. No one seemed to notice me standing there with my two children. Each daughter had their arms wrapped around one of my legs. They were trembling in fear. I was glad we weren't in the crowd so that we weren't close to danger, but as I looked down into the deep, murky waters I saw prehistoric fish circling my island of rock. They were looking up at us hoping one of us would accidentally quiver and fall in so they could devour us. This dream has stayed with me and was extremely disturbing. In a way, it mirrored what I was experiencing in my personal life where I felt nowhere was safe. I felt that I was on an island alone with my kids and that if I made one wrong move, I would plummet along with my children to a place where would be devoured. Small town living in the midst of a crisis is a blessing and a curse.

HOWEVER, things were looking up and I just didn't realize it.

I got my PRAXIS scores back and found out that I passed, not only did I pass, I passed above average, THE FIRST TIME. I had heard of so many not passing their tests and having to take it multiple times. I was just so relieved when I found out I had passed. It meant that I was employable…as a teacher!

CHAPTER FOURTEEN

It was time for Anna's 6th birthday party. Now, I believe birthday parties are a big deal, a celebration of life, things completed, and experiences yet to come. I was exhausted from the surroundings of life at that time. I mean, how do you celebrate a birthday with happiness and joy if you are not happy and joyful? I resigned to doing a small party so as not to disappoint.

I don't know if I have mentioned it yet, but I was not the cook in the family. When Michael Ray and I first married, he was at work during his internship at the college and he called me and asked me to make him some food and bring it to him. Of course, like any young wife, I obliged. Now, you see, I had been living in a dorm and then with my grandmother, I hadn't had too many opportunities to cook and to make food. I surveyed the kitchen and found some things that I thought would be good to eat (at the time). I scurried around and whipped up some tuna salad and macaroni and cheese. Yes, I know that doesn't sound like a great dinner, but it was what we had and I can promise you, it was put together with love and care. I packed it all up and drove it to the gymnasium where he was. I remember giving it to him and he said, "What is this?" I told him that it was his dinner. As he walked away with it, I heard some remarks about not letting me cook anymore and so I kind of just stopped. I didn't spend my first year as a young wife in the kitchen attempting to make a new meal each night; I patiently waited for Michael Ray to get home so he could fix what he wanted. We finally settled into a routine of how this would be and all the wounded feelings left as it became our new routine. He was the cook and I was not. This is how it went until he left. I know I've mentioned something about cereal being dinner once or twice in the depressed times, but I had finally gotten a small grip on the kitchen. As Anna's birthday arrived, we settled on each daughter inviting a friend to spend the night. Now, since I am the one who loves giving a big birthday party, I had always done the cake coordinating whether it was a friend buying the cake or it was ordering the cake. This year was the year I made a cake! I set out a Tinkerbell cake complete with pastel confetti and a Tinkerbell topper. I was so proud of that cake and I believe that my girls were as well as they knew that this was something I had never done before.

Anna's birthday was another thing that made finality of our family of four evident. Birthday parties had always involved all of the family members of both sides of the family to come together to celebrate this child. It brought together grandparents who squished on the couch together to see the child open the extravagant gifts that were purchased with nothing but love and pride. These were times when someone was around to take a picture of all four of us and on this particular birthday, it was up to me to make this day special for this little girl. I remember asking Michael Ray what he was going to do and it was as if the family had already decided, unbeknownst to me, that they would have a celebration for her on one of his weekends. This was the beginning of my children not having both of their parents around for everything.

Anna's birthday came and went and soon came Easter. I did as I had always done and attempted to coordinate our outfits. I made sure that the girls were with me on Easter as I couldn't bear being without them just yet. The colors for us that year were hot pink, black and white. I had bought the girls matching dresses and put my best face forward and drove them to church. We sat together as a little threesome and then I noticed, from the back of the church, their dad slipped in. I tried to keep my best face on and not let that deter the message that I needed that day. After church was over, my friend Kim took a picture of the three of us in our coordinated Easter outfits while he stood and looked over from a distance. The girls ran to him and hugged him; someone took their picture together, and then it was time to go. I had held it together. I had made it. We had a new pastor who had preached that morning and he was aware of my situation. I made an appointment to visit with him at some point during the week. Later that day, I drove the girls to my father's for an Easter Egg Hunt. It was nice to get to be there and not have to think too much. My dad was very kind to me during this time. I received lots of hugs, chocolate bunnies and laughs that day.

I did go see the pastor later that week and I have never been so disheartened in meeting with a man of God. Rather than soothing my soul (which was all I really needed at the time), I was shown scripture about divorce situations. His interpretation was very definitive for him and involved using the words adultery. I left feeling angry and hurt. I was used to being in a ministering role to other women. I knew that I was a woman who needed love and acceptance spoken into her very being and not doctrine. I was angry and I did talk about this with a few members of the church. Ultimately, I felt the need to move to a new place where I knew I would be embraced and welcomed no matter where I came from, and I knew in my heart that is the kind of church Christ wants His people to be. I was beginning to let go of old things that weren't purposely holding me back but did not permit me to grow. Right or wrong, the divorce was happening whether I wanted it to or not. The label of divorcée and single mom were enough without adding the word adultery to my list.

Libby Sears Blair

CHAPTER FIFTEEN

Soon after Easter, a huge Kentucky "holiday" was approaching. I looked at my calendar enough in advance to see that Michael Ray would have the girls and I wanted to be a part of Derby! I was free to go to Louisville, spend time with Tammy and just be free to be me. I actually researched horses that were running in the race and knew which horse I wanted to win. I let Tammy choose where we would go and what we would do because I really didn't know Louisville that well yet. I set out in my gold Malibu and drove to Louisville. I was wearing black strappy heels, dark blue jeans, a white shirt and a black flowy sweater over top. I was happy. I'm not sure where we were but we ate outdoors at some little café type bar. There was a fountain and a courtyard. When it was time for the race, we went inside the bar to watch the Derby. My horse didn't win; I think he was second (I don't even remember his name). There was really no one around, but I didn't care. I was with my friend whom I could tell anything to, and I really thought that I was living it up. Since, in later years, having been more involved in the Derby Celebration, I now realize that she was humoring me and taking me to a place where I could relax and have a good time while still feeling like I was celebrating. We walked down the street in our heels and went into a unique little dive in the Highlands of Louisville where there hangs a wall spread of a picture of Burt Reynolds, naked! She took my photo with this iconic picture and we laughed and laughed. Looking back at the pictures of this day, I almost want to cry not because of a horse, or a beer garden or of Burt Reynolds, but because I was inwardly happy. New Life was springing forth inside of me.

The following day, I drove to Shelbyville to go to church with my mom and step-dad and then out to eat. Over the past ten years, their life has been in a state of flux as well, but this day was a good day. We enjoyed dinner together and spent some time riding around on a Sunday drive. We visited a property that they owned next door to the house where I was raised. It was a little one-bedroom efficiency apartment that was transformed from an old early 1900's carriage house. I was impressed with the progress that had been made, for all I could remember from my youth was an old broken down building. There were a few boyfriends that I would take to the other side so that we couldn't be seen. I remember leaning up against the old wood while talking to a boy or kissing and as I opened my eyes from the kiss I could see the broken windows and the old things that were inside. We, my brother and sister as well as the neighborhood kids and sometimes the boys I was with, wondered what was inside that old building. Now it had all been cleaned out and it was a perfect little spot for someone who might want to have a weekend getaway near Taylorsville Lake.

My parents showed me the inside of the property. I couldn't get cell service inside the room so I ventured out on the steps to sit and called my girls, after all, it was Mother's Day. This was the first Mother's Day without my girls. When I was a social worker, I used to have foster kids' mothers call and have a special request to see their child on Mother's Day. Honestly, part of me scoffed at their request because they hadn't done something right as a mother and what, now they wanted to be mother of the year? Well, it didn't work that way for them, but I was very different than they. I would never hurt one of my girls or neglect them in any way, and yet, my girls were pulled from me on this very day. When I called them, they were so excited and told me all about everything going on. I talked to their father for a moment, expecting him to say Happy Mother's Day. Somehow, I believed he owed me that, but he never did say it. I could hear many of my in laws in the background and, like a knife, it hit me that I would no longer be a part of that family in the same way that I had been. Things were changing and I was trying so hard to let go. It is hard to let go when your knuckles are white from trying to hold on for so long.

In the days after Derby and Mother's Day, Michael Ray and I began to see a lawyer. We began to divide belongings. We were civil. I don't think I was even mad at this point. I was determined to make the legal part as easy as possible. To this very day, there have been very few legal issues that we have not been able to resolve. We were sitting in the lawyer's office and the lawyer mentioned out loud how diplomatic we were being about everything and somehow, that was a blow to my heart. I was only being diplomatic because I had to be. I didn't see any good of being nasty or spiteful in the divorce proceedings. This is not to say that I didn't want to be mean and try to take everything. This is not also to say that I didn't want to get up and scream at everyone, "This isn't the way that my life is supposed to go! I'm not supposed to be divorcing and becoming a single mother!" Many of the legalities had to wait on the ramifications of the horrible thing to run their course, therefore the divorce did not happen as quickly as I would have liked for closure's sake.

My Master's graduation was quickly approaching. I was a little lost at how to handle this event. I struggled with wanting Michael Ray to be there as he had for so many things before and not want to have him there at all. I knew my mother and step dad would be in Houston at a previously scheduled engagement and my dad and his wife wouldn't drive after dark, so the audience for my momentous occasion was looking sparse. My dad and his wife decided to join me for dinner before the graduation ceremony. The lifesaver of the evening was Tammy. She and her four children drove two hours to my University to sit through Amazing Grace sung operatic style, hear my name rattled over the speaker, watch me try not to trip in my heels as I shook the President's hand and received my degree. Tammy stayed with my two girls and I had my own little fan club in the back of the chapel. I am always grateful for this night. Though there were not very many loved ones there, there was so much love. This night began to bring back a little pride that had been robbed the night of the horrible thing. I felt accomplished and that feeling made me know I was capable of doing more things on my own.

With this new sense of achievement, I was able to make it through the last weeks of the school year in the classroom in which I worked. As school was ending, I knew there were possibilities for the future, though at this time I did not know what they would be. I also did not know that the ramifications of the horrible thing would begin swirling around me once again, yet the demons were rearing their ugly head.

CHAPTER
SIXTEEN

My birthday is June 2nd, which, ironically, happened to be the closing day of school. It had been a miserable school year in that building where daily, I saw the man that I had made lifelong vows to walk right past me without ever saying anything day in and day out. I was glad that the year was ending. As we loaded the special education students in wheelchairs and walked them to the bus for the last time that school year, it completely hit me that I had no idea what I was going to do. When I came to the classroom to pack up my belongings, I began to cry because I had no idea what was next.

In true Libby fashion, I had given enough thought to my birthday to plan a big party for myself so that I wouldn't be alone on that date. I had sent out an invitation to my girlfriends to meet me for hibachi. I recall that I had sold something in the garage that would have been considered a mutual belonging for $100. He had asked if he could come to the restaurant and pick up his $50. I sent his cash out with a friend so that I didn't have to go out into the parking lot and be upset on the night I was celebrating my birthday. He went on about his business after that and it would be many days later that I would find out more horrible things. As my girlfriends and I were ordering fun drinks, catching shrimp in our mouths and watching our chef create the onion volcano, the underlying lava in the lithosphere of my life was getting ready to spew again and I was just beginning to have fun and realize I was okay.

I want to take a moment before I describe the new eruption that was getting ready to take place and say something about friends. In my life, I've been blessed with so many friends. Just the idea that beautiful souls took time out of their lives during parts of this windy road I travelled is exhilarating. One sweet soul, in particular asked me a few weeks prior to my birthday what my favorite bible verse was and I shared this verse with her "Blessed are those whose strength is in you, whose hearts are set on pilgrimage," Psalm 84:5. Little did I know that she was taking that verse and making me a beautifully etched picture to be hung in my home. This craft is a prized possession in my home even today. It represents two things to me: the first being that friends will always be willing to do things like this for you and they are truly the joys in life and are unexpected treasures, the second is the focus on the word pilgrimage. When I was young and in private Christian school we read John Bunyan's Pilgrim's Progress. I always appreciated the text for the allegories in the writing. What I remember most about the book was Christian's journey and how he encountered all of the other characters on the road. The verse says pilgrimage. Pilgrimage is nothing more than a journey. This verse hangs in my home and serves as a reminder of the journey that I daily walk and that the only way I can keep my heart right on my journey is to get my strength daily from God. That strength is sometimes delivered in the form of beautiful friendships.

Back to the volcano eruption, in the coming days, I would learn more about the horrible thing than I actually wanted to know. I think that learning more about the events that led up to the horrible thing helped me focus on moving forward. My heartbreak was not as strong, though still present, and I was beginning to see things with clearer eyes. When heartbreak settles, you begin to take the focus off of the other person and what they did or did not do and focus on helping yourself. This particular summer was the one summer that I began to grow as a person, individually. I made decisions by myself for my children and myself without consulting Michael Ray as he was not going to be a part of the inner workings of my life in the future. I don't share details of the horrible thing out of respect for Michael Ray's life because my intention is to let you know how I came out of a horrible thing and began walking on my own. I will share that during this time, as I was beginning to get stronger and healthier, I believe that he was walking in his darkest days. It was so very hard to separate myself from someone that, daily, I had cared for, someone that I had made vows to love and protect, but for my own mental health and self-preservation, I had to let him walk his own walk as I was walking my own as well. I didn't do this easily. I am a person that will hold on to what I care about until it absolutely needs to be let go. After living several years past this time, I do much better with that, but at the time this was happening, it was a daily struggle to let go. Some days I let go very well and focused on myself and other days I was pulled into the mire of his darkness. In those dark times, I learned more about choices that had led to where we were. I learned how I had been lied to, devalued and disrespected. It would be later before I would learn that the opinions of others do not influence who I am.

The molten lava that spewed from the volcano that was my life for the past six months was slowing. It was still hot and occasionally burned deep. I had a focus on moving forward and finding a job. I was a certified teacher in the state of Kentucky with no students or school. Daily, I swam laps to take care of my health. I was losing weight even though I wasn't focused on weight loss, I was more focused on health and being healthy for my children. I learned that the healthier I was physically, the healthier I also was mentally. Every morning I woke to a scripture and prayer time to keep my heart right. I let God take care of me, cradle me and move me in the direction in which He wanted me.

Libby Sears Blair

CHAPTER
SEVENTEEN

On the morning of June 22, 2011, I prayed simply for something beautiful to happen in my life and I told God that he could decide what that would be. Now, a side note about this prayer, I wish I could tell you that I pray this often, that I am always living in the will of God so solidly that I just let Him decide everything for me, but I really struggle with this. I wish that, even today as I write this, I were as fearless as I was this day. You see, I had nothing to lose and everything to gain.

This is the prayer as it is written in my journal:

June 22, 2011

Lord,

Each day I am further from the pain I felt in November of 2010 and for that, I am grateful. I see promise and possibility in the future, although I really don't know where I will be in two months. I feel like a senior in high school who doesn't know what to do when graduating.

I am finally calm in this storm as it continues to rage with Michael Ray losing his job. Lord, I am content to go wherever You put me. I don't know why I am drawn to Shelbyville so much other than the fact that I have good solid memories from there.

Lord, I ask You to open doors for my children and I to have provision from you. Please open my eyes to all that you want to offer me. Please keep my mind focused on you and press all that I know about You into my heart.

God, Thank you so much for Tammy and the gift that she is to my children and me. You are so evident in her life. Lord, help me find a teaching job somewhere.

God, now that I have broken down the whirlwind of thoughts inside my head, I still pray, pray, pray for my girls; that I am taking care of them and meeting their needs and that I am seeing what they need immediately. Lord, I ask that they be untouched by the situation at hand, that they be excited if they were to find out we are moving and that You claim every step that they make in life.

Lord, I know that I say I am tired of being strong, but I am. I just ask for a time and a place that I can touch into my female side and be the weaker sex who is taken care of. I always pray for Michael Ray too, so of course, I lift him up to You. I am pulling away from him when he needs this person to talk to because that is not my place anymore. I ask that you give him good solid friends and find control within. I also ask that he is able to find a job and be the male role model he should be.

God, I just ask that the things I have a hard heart about become a distant memory and that I wouldn't even know those feelings anymore unless they are for Your glory.

I just keep praying for something beautiful. Lord, what that is, is up to You.

Love,

Libby

Within an hour after praying this prayer, I was on the phone with the principal at Shelby West Middle School in my hometown of Shelbyville, Kentucky. I had not really ruled out anywhere at this point because I needed to work. I knew moving back to the Shelbyville area would be where my heart was. I also obtained an interview at North Hardin High School in Hardin County, Kentucky.

Over the course of the next few days, I interviewed both places. The day that I was to interview in Shelby County, I sent my girls off with a friend, arose early, got in my little gold car, and began the hour and half drive to Shelbyville. About an hour before the interview, I was still about half hour away from my destination, and not one tire, but two tires completely blew out on the freeway. I was dressed as nicely as I could be for the interview and now, here I was on the side of the road minutes before an interview that could change my life and not sure how to get there. Good thing I had left with plenty of time to spare. I called my step-dad and he actually happened to be within proximity enough to come and pick me up and take me to the interview. I arrived on time to a dark school. Apparently, there had been a storm the night before that had left West Middle without lights and had left debris on the road. I would later figure out that the debris on the freeway was what had caused my tires to blow. I was able to pull myself together and sit in a dark room with a principal I had never met and rattle off answers about literacy strategies, relationships with children, classroom management and such. Before the interview was over, she said YES! She welcomed me to the school and told me that I was now a Warrior. (haha, I already knew that!) She said that she would not be able to offer me an official contract until July 1st, however it was a verbal commitment. I wanted to be away from Hodgenville, away from all of the molten lava. The next day, I interviewed at North Hardin High School. I had another good interview there. I felt good about the positivity and the fact that some things were looking brighter than before.

That afternoon, I received a call from the principal from North Hardin High School in Radcliff, Kentucky who offered me a position at his school. He said to me that I might not know everything about teaching, but he could tell that I was able to have relationships with others and that is not something you can teach a new teacher, either they have it or they don't. He said that he could teach me everything else I needed to know. This was asserting to hear and I needed affirming things to happen in my life. I did tell him that I had already been offered a job with Shelby County Public Schools. He asked if I had a contract and I said no, but I would have one next month. He said that was bull and that he could produce one on the spot. I asked if I could call him back and of course, he said yes. I then called

Shelby County Schools and told them that Hardin County Schools was offering me a contract that day. Within hours a contract had been faxed to me from Shelby County Schools. I was official and much sooner than I had expected.

After having graduated with my Master's, this was another feat that I had accomplished and needed to be crossed off my list. However, by crossing this accomplishment off my list, it opened the door for many more items to be added to the list. My head was spinning, I would be moving, but where? What would I do with the house that I currently lived in? My children, my precious babies, how were they going to handle all of the changes that I was currently recognizing were going to be a reality? There were even the heartstrings that made me wonder how Michael Ray was going to take the news and did he care if we left?

CHAPTER
EIGHTEEN

I was to begin work in late July. I had approximately one month before I needed to be in a new home and reporting to the new job. I faced the confusion of trying to live in one place and owning a home in another. I knew that since I had house payments to make in Hodgenville, I would need to live very modestly for a time until I could release myself of that obligation. I talked with Tammy about this (I talked to her about everything) and she offered her basement for the girls and I to room in. I was agreeable to this because I had to be. I didn't know of any other choices. She said that until I got the house sold, I could stay with her rent-free because she understood that I wouldn't be able to make it financially. I was very excited about this and also looking forward to having a partner to help me do life just as I would be able to help her.

The week of July 4th came about and I ended up spending the week with Tammy. During the week with her I was excited to see an old friend that I had not seen in many years and much of the week revolved around the reality that we may be in each other's lives again. I was busy in her home, helping with whatever, thinking about what it would be like to move in with her and for this to be "home" for a while. I was very excited with all of the new possibilities though I admit; I noticed Tammy was hard to "land" to talk to about the upcoming move. I was taking care of her kiddos during the daytime as well as my own while she was working. We celebrated July 4th as a group on the banks of the Ohio River. We sat and watched about seven fireworks shows while the kids played on old playground equipment. We ate fish and chips and relaxed.

The next day, I was extremely anxious because the meeting with my old friend was to occur that evening. I had made arrangements for my girls to be picked up by my parents so that I was free for the evening. I was looking forward to a day of reflection before I went out that night; however, a very scary thing happened. My dog, Rudy, disappeared. Now, keep in mind, while Tammy was working, there were Tammy's four children and my two so, a very anxious, clueless woman was taking care of six children by herself. It was about ten o'clock in the morning and I noticed that I hadn't seen the dog in a few minutes. By the time that I quizzed each child, I was able to conclude that the youngest of the children had opened the front door to let her out of the house and she had let the dog out as well. By ten twenty, in lieu of a shower, I had all six children walking the entire neighborhood with me as I frantically called for Rudy. We walked up and down each street in a neighborhood in which I didn't even live. We stopped every runner and mother pushing a stroller. No one had seen him. I was worried that he had made it to the main highway and had been picked up by Louisville Metro Animal Control. Not knowing what to do next, I put all six children in my Tammy's Pathfinder and we visited every Humane Society and Animal Shelter that I could find in the Louisville Listings. I barely recall one of the children in a dress up costume of a princess and another without shoes on as I had rushed them into the car. Melody always laughs when we talk about this day because she remembers how disheveled we looked and how, at one shelter, when we showed up, a news crew was there. It was fee free adoption day for cats and apparently a news crew was hoping to do a story on a child getting a new kitten. I was in no mood to have a camera shoved in my face or explain to the masses that I hadn't had a shower and that typically I make sure children have shoes on. (The princess dress was a common occurrence, but my lack of shower and shoeless children were not.) I quickly tried to maneuver past the cameras and ask if this shelter had seen our sweet little dog. No shelter that we implored had seen Rudy. I was dying on the inside. I finally had done all I could do except for reach out on social media. I made a post that sounded like this: Libby Sears Blair is not having a very good day. We are visiting a friend in Louisville and my dog, Rudy left their house this morning...we noticed about 20 minutes after he was gone...cannot find him anywhere. Have been searching all morning, drove around everywhere looking for him, talked to stroller pushers, runners, garbage people, been to Animal Control and the Humane Society. I'm sick about it. I hope he shows up."

My cousin Laura, whom you will remember had given me the treasured family items at Christmas saw the post and offered to make posters to help me hang up in the Louisville area. I also called The Courier-Journal and placed an ad describing Rudy as a lost dog in need of his family. It truly felt like I had lost a child of my own. About four o'clock that day we got a knock at the door that was a lead. She said that a lady who lives in the neighborhood, with a dark Honda picked him up this morning and checked in the neighborhood to see if he belonged to anyone. I finally began to calm down thinking I would soon know where my little Rudy was. Tammy arrived home from work about four thirty and I removed myself from the children and took a moment for myself on the front steps. As I was sitting there, a dark Honda pulled up in the driveway and asked if I was the one who had been looking for the dog. I said yes. She got Rudy out of her car and he immediately ran into my arms and laid his head on my shoulder, not easing up in intensity and snuggling at all. She said that was all she needed to see to know that he was mine. As she and I talked, I learned that he had wandered into her driveway as she was leaving for work. She did not have enough time to attempt to find his owner since she was going to work so she put him in her basement for the day until she returned home. I thanked her over and over again.

I began to realize that if I lived at Tammy's I would not be able to keep Rudy with me as this could happen many more times in a house with six children. I called my dad up and explained the day's events to him and asked if he would take Rudy. His beloved shih tzu had recently passed away and I thought he might be open to having a similar type dog around in his place. I decided that I should go on and take Rudy to him instantly so there would be no more issues and Rudy would be in safety. I quickly told Tammy what I was doing and I loaded the girls up in my car along with Rudy and all of his belongings. We made the trip from Louisville to Mount Washington in a short time. I remember thinking that would be a bonus to living at Tammy's because I was not used to being that close to my dad's house before.

It was hard to give up Rudy, but after a day of worrying about him lost in the city, I knew he would be happier living with my dad out in the open. My dad certainly seemed happy. On the way back, I was exhausted, in need of a shower and was beginning to hear from my friend...did I still want to get together tonight? Did I have any ideas where to meet up? My mind was beginning to shift back to my evening plans. I had to get the girls to my mom to spend the night and then try to calm down and focus on what the night would be.

After sending the girls on to my mom's for the night, I went back to Tammy's for the shower that I had intended on taking about ten that morning. When I walked in, the house was very quiet. Her children's father had picked the four of them up. She was working in the kitchen on some emails and such and I was finally going to get ready for the night ahead.

Then, of all things, it hit. I remember kind of being chatty in the kitchen and explaining why it made sense to give Rudy to my dad especially since I was moving into her house. That's when she stopped and said the words that I didn't quite understand. She said, "I don't think it is going to work out." I wasn't sure exactly what she meant wasn't going to work out. She had seemed so sure that she wanted to offer her home to me to stay in. I believed her. At this moment, I realized that there was no one on Earth I could believe. If I couldn't believe Tammy, I could believe no one. She was the closest thing to honesty and truth that I knew of and now she was reneging on the plan that had been her idea. It had already been a long, hard day. A day, in which, at the end, I had lost, found and then given away my dog and now I am supposed to see a man I've not seen in ten years which I am most apprehensive about as well as come to the reality that I accepted a job based on a place to live and now I do not have a place to live. No husband. No money. No home. No dog. Yet, I was still getting texts from Bruce asking me what time I could be ready. Man, that shower sounded even better at this point. Instead of taking a shower, I lost it. I think I really momentarily lost my mind. I yelled, I screamed, I cursed and I didn't care. I was angry, so angry that I had to leave the conversation and get in the damn shower.

I was getting a divorce, my still husband was facing legal charges for the horrible thing, I was going to see someone that night that I hadn't seen in years, I was moving (somewhere), I was starting a new job, I had just given up my dog. If I had one more change in another twenty-four hour period, it was likely that my head would explode, I feared. I was soon in a presentable shape. I left Tammy's house for what would end up being all night long. The next morning as I was going to my car, she began calling my cell phone. I told her I was fine and that I had just spent a long night catching up. Ten years is a lot to try to learn about someone in one night.

I got the children, returned to Tammy's, gathered my belongings and went back to Hodgenville sans dog. What should have been a good beginning ended up breaking my heart just a little more. I couldn't talk to her. I didn't have the words or the energy. Things were happening faster than I could handle. I remember calling my mom and explaining that now that I have a job in Shelby County, I have no home. If you will recall, there is a little carriage house that my parents (my mom and step-dad) owned that was right next to my childhood home. It had been renovated as an efficiency apartment for one. I can't remember the term of endearment that my mother had for the place, but in my mind, it was a shack. Yes, a shack. It was a one-bedroom apartment for my two girls and me. The only thing that was great about it was that it was free and within driving distance to my new job. Of course mom offered it to us and I took the offer. Beggars can't be choosers and I needed to get out of Hodgenville.

CHAPTER NINETEEN

In the days ahead, things did not slow down. I lived in a seventeen hundred square foot home and every inch of it had to be packed up and moved one hundred miles. To say I was overwhelmed was an understatement. The week of Vacation Bible School at the church that I was not happy with occurred the same week that much of my packing needed to occur. As much as I had my issues with the church, my girls had friends there, so nightly, I took them to Vacation Bible School and I packed. I had not talked with Tammy since I left her house because I was hurt and I didn't know what to say. Each night a different friend had come to the house to help me pack. One phone call had been from Tammy who thought that she had time to drive to Hodgenville to help me pack. I am not mean spirited even when someone has hurt me and so I accepted her help. I didn't have the energy to fight or be angry. There were enough changes going on without losing your best friend. I needed the help, so when she got there, we set to work in Melody's room which seemed to be the hardest room of the entire house. Melody's room was tedious due to all of the toys and needs of an eight year old. We didn't really talk about big things but we did get big things done and then she had to leave. I made peace with the situation. I've noticed over the years, that when Tammy and I enter a zone of contention it is easier to let it go than force a huge discussion because we do love each other. (Since the time that this was initially written, I have discussed this situation with Tammy again. She reminded me that there had been flooding in the basement and that is why she couldn't offer her home to me as she had originally planned. I told her that I had not really comprehended that fact until years later. I'm sure she explained it, but all that I heard, at the time was that she offered me a place to stay and then it was pulled out from underneath me.)

Slowly things came together. I had a large yard sale, which my friends were calling my divorce sale. I sold all of my primitive décor. I couldn't look at all of the sweet little pieces that said "family" and "love" on them, so they were out the door.

Like most days I live, I have this innate philosophy inside of me that says, "Okay, I'll try again tomorrow," and so I did. The next day was a new day and the house was starting to look more like a shell with boxes rather than a home. Each day came with more packing until the whole house was complete. Looking back, it feels like I did it all by myself, but I know that isn't the case. Every day or so someone would come by to help. Ultimately, I was the orchestrator of the move and some way, somehow, things began to make it from Hodgenville to Little Mount, to my storage unit or to my little shack.

On the day that the last load was to be brought, on the day that we would find ourselves sleeping in Little Mount rather than Hodgenville, more of the horrible thing revealed itself. The horrible thing was live on the news that night and in print in the papers that day. Everywhere I had my little girls, I was assessing for safety. I was protecting my babies from what they might see that would change the view of their father and wash away their innocence. As dear servant friends helped us make that last trip, as I loaded my car (which was on its last leg) to the brim, we drove to Little Mount. We somehow avoided the news story of the day.

As I awoke the next morning in a one-bedroom apartment, which was to be my home, as I looked around and gathered my thoughts, I was completely overwhelmed. We had no gas, so the stove was not in working order. My dad's wife had given me a hot plate to use and I also had a microwave. The bathroom was larger than the kitchen and we had a small couch and desk in another nook of the place.

On July 28, 2011, I was officially moved. Since the small shack was next door to where I grew up as a child, I took comfort in walking outside into the back yard and feeling some peace and comfort. I had never felt so right about what I had done but so alone in the process in my life. The grass was green every morning and I knew deep in my heart that God's promises were too. I had just enough days ahead to get organized, to figure out the girls' new dress code at school and begin my job.

As normal, I plowed ahead. Looking back on all those fully packed days, I know that God gave me the strength to keep going. There were still residuals of the horrible thing, but I was building a new home and wasn't allowing those things into my life. I'm not sure when my health became super important to me, but throughout this time, I started to eat right and take care of myself. I think the main reason was that I knew I was all that my girls had and that they needed me to be healthy to take care of them. We got a membership at the local Family Activity Center where they could swim and I could work out.

I know money was an issue, but isn't it interesting that it is not the thing that I focus upon when telling this story? It is likely I had none or very little but I don't seem to remember because daily, all of my needs were met. Though I didn't want to live in the little shack, it was becoming home; even sharing a bed with Anna, even with the bed being on a slanted floor, even though my back hurt nightly, it was our home. August 6th would be the next time since June that I would sit down with my prayer journal and consider my journey.

Libby Sears Blair

CHAPTER
TWENTY

Lord,

As I read the last entry, I think of all that has transpired. I want to give You all the glory for answered prayers in the midst of my still raging storm. There have been some very hard days, some extremely sad days and some heart breaking days but I am seeing the rewards of faithfulness time and time again.

You, Lord, are beautiful, faithful and true to your daughter. When all else fails, I can truly depend on You. It is not foolish to bank on the maker of the stars.

When I was last able to sit down and write, I was so uncertain about where I would be in the future. I was uncertain about a job and a move. Lord, You have orchestrated everything so beautifully. You provided a home, a safe haven from all that transpired with Michael Ray, You have provided a job, a focus and a move. Thank You for all the people that literally showed up at my home to help me move.

Thank You for helping me with my girls day in and day out. Thank You for meeting my heart's desires for them; that they would have a good education and opportunities.

Lord, forgive me when I lose patience, when I am worried or stressed. Help me to remember I am shielding them from this grown up world for a reason and I don't need them to see worry or fear in me. They need to see a momma dependent upon You.

Lord, be with their sweet hearts as they begin school in a new place. I ask that you introduce them to good friends, playmates who are loyal and trustworthy to them.

Lord, thank you that my first two work days went smoothly. I have enjoyed meeting people and you have affirmed for me once again that I am in the right place. I ask a special blessing over this team I will be working with this year as well as the school, the students and the leadership. Help me be a part of a system that operates with integrity and the best interest of the children. Help me listen and learn and do things the right way. Help me be assertive when I need to be but also mindful when it would be best not to address an issue. Lord, please give me discernment in my new job.

Also, Lord, I am asking for discernment in other areas. I am asking for financial discernment from things as little as staying away from a purchase I don't need as big as what to do about my house and how to prioritize what needs to be done financially while meeting all of our needs.

Thank You Lord that You are a Father that I can tell all of my thoughts and feelings to. You know them anyway. Lord, Your creation, in its purest form, is beautiful and I desire to lend to its value.

I almost want to avoid the next part of my prayer because you have heard this from my heart over and over in the past few days. Lord, I pray that you are with Michael Ray as he deals with his consequences of the horrible thing. I pray that you give him the strength to work through the demons that want to take over his mind. Please take care of him, keep him safe and begin new works in him. Lord, be with his family as they are walking alongside him on this bleak road. Reach down and strengthen them.

Thank You for today Jesus. Thank You for rest, reflection and promises of hope and future in You. I love You Lord with every ounce of my being.

Lift me up to be strong and have peace in the strength, humbly I pray.

Amen,

Libby

The first two days on the job were "new teacher orientation" where I sat in a room with other new and aspiring teachers or among those who had moved their teaching practices to this district. I was grateful to be in the room where administrators were talking about the most important values of education in the district. I met a few of the teachers that I would be working with and was invited to a Back to School Cookout at one of the teacher's houses. It was nice to be included. Over the next several days, I attended meeting after meeting which immersed me into Shelby County Public Schools. Since I am a Specific Learning Disability teacher, I was to collaborate and teach in Science, Math and Reading that school year. There was a math professional development where I was to go and learn how to teach math to special needs kids. The instructors taught the class with very high-level math to demonstrate how it must feel for a student who lacks the ability to learn mathematical functions. If I disconnect with rocket science type math, then a student who can't understand a simple concept will disconnect as well. The professional development was helpful and good for me as a teacher, but with all I was going through personally with the move and the drama of the summer, it was extremely difficult for me to attempt to stretch my mind as far as I was stretching it.

During the Back to School Cookout, I met a few people who would become pivotal in my life in a very short time. This was a cookout at the librarian's house. It was the first time that I was meeting co-workers outside of meetings. We were to bring a dish, which was a little scary for me, because I wasn't sure what to prepare in my kitchen with no working stove. I finally bought everything I needed to make a refrigerated chocolate éclair. I knew I could pass as having a nice dessert to share that way and it was one that didn't have to be cooked.

When I walked in with my dessert, there was another teacher there who had brought the same dessert. She just laughed and laughed at the thought of having two of the same desserts! Good, I thought, I fit in. I remember thinking how important that was for me to be able to feel normal. None of these people knew a thing about my personal hell that I had endured. While this was a blessing and a new start, it was also scary how I didn't know who to be in this new world. Little did I know that God had that all figured out. My children were freely running around in Chellie's backyard and I was resting on the patio with a cup of iced tea. Across from me sat a very sweet teacher who asked me who was doing my KTIP. KTIP stands for Kentucky Teacher Internship Program and it is something that every new teacher is required to do during his or her first year in teaching. In the KTIP program, an experienced teacher mentors the new teacher. I replied that I didn't know who would be doing that. This chick seemed to have it all together. Within minutes, she had texted the principal to ask if she could be my mentor and had taken me under her wing. She was to be my mentor for KTIP. At the time I didn't know what a blessing that was. I now know how important she was in my life even on that very night. Melissa became a true friend immediately as did Sophie, the chocolate éclair twin.

We had a day or two off to recover from all of the professional development that I dove right into after the move. I spent the last little bit of time loving on my girls and unpacking. I was trying to put in order some of the chaos that surrounded me figuratively and literally. I wasn't really apprehensive as the first day of school was right around the corner for us. I guess I was ready to see students. If there is one thing I always do right, it is kids. I can talk to kids, work with kids and be with kids. Melody and Anna pretty much hung on my every move. They are such sweet, resilient little girls. I like to think that I gave them the tools they needed to do well.

CHAPTER
TWENTY-ONE

The morning of the first day of school, I treated it like I always have and had them stand together and take pictures. I didn't want the shack to show in the pictures so I had them stand where the background in the pictures was the old house in which I was raised. Life really does come full circle because, ironically enough, they stood in the very same place that I used to stand and wait for the bus when I was a little girl. After a brief picture session, I put all three of us in the car and whisked us away to Shelbyville. The girls were going to elementary school and I was going to middle school. I was very happy that their building was right next to mine and that they were allowed to ride the bus from one place to the next without any transportation issues.

The very first day of school, the students stayed in their homerooms most of the time, so I was asked to meet with other special education teachers and do certain paperwork that needs to be completed in the first few days of school. I remember one particular instance where we were in a room checking students' schedules to ensure that they were in the right classes and we were having some small talk. There was one teacher there that had been a former teammate of Michael Ray's on the college football team. He had gone through a divorce and was newly remarried. He was one person who knew my personal hell. He was also one who had met me at the storage unit to help me unload my things. He was just asking how things were generally and

I mentioned that I was frustrated with the drive to drop off and pick up kids. There was another teacher in the room and I guess she had overheard our conversation. She nodded and said, "You do what you've gotta do." I had no idea what that meant at the time, but she was wiser than I knew. Though Claire didn't know my particular story, I would soon find out that I had nothing to complain about as she sends her children out west for an entire summer and also loses them at Christmas due to a divorce decree. At that moment, my world was so big and everyone else's so small, I couldn't really fathom that anyone had it worse or even the same as I did. Through listening to others tell their stories, my own didn't seem quite so big.

God really knew what he was doing. He placed me into the very arms of people who had been through very similar circumstances. Through Claire, Sophie and Melissa, I learned that I wasn't as different as Hodgenville would have made me out to be and that with them I had a family and support. Can you believe it? Another something beautiful coming from the horrible thing?

I often look back and reference my friendships at West as my divorce support group. God knows that we needed each other. They each became pivotal in my survival and growth. I saw how other strong single women made their lives work and along with Tammy's example, it became clearer that I could do it too. Those first few weeks as a teacher in my new job, I felt as though I was drowning. It was all I could do to get up, get kids ready, go to work and then come home, attempt cooking some sort of dinner in the thing I called a kitchen and go to bed. I wanted to work out, but I couldn't make myself muster up the energy to do so.

Anna seemed to have the hardest time adjusting. Maybe it was because she was so young, but there were times when she was not able to express herself so she would cry. She would cry for a very long time. Many nights after I had completed all of the day's worth of responsibilities, just as I was ready to crawl into bed, knowing it would start all over the next day; this would be the time that she would begin to cry. I'm not talking just a little crying, I'm talking like, for two hours until she fell asleep. I didn't know what to do except hold her. Some nights she would wail that she missed Mrs. Bray, her kindergarten teacher. Other nights she would cry that she missed her daddy. It wore on me as the night approached because I never knew quite sure what night was going to be the night that would not end in peace but in tears. I shared this with her teachers at school and they were wonderful about being that extra support that I needed to parent my child.

One of the things I quickly learned was that I had to have a village. I didn't want a village at first. I wasn't used to asking for help and it felt so very foreign to me. I was used to Michael Ray and I figuring out what to do for the children.

Tammy and I thought it would be helpful to my girls in this new place if they visited sometimes just to ease the newness of it and make it feel more like home if there were guests around us. One night in particular, she brought all four of her children to my house and I made dinner from our little kitchen. I will never know what struck a chord with Anna, but she began to cry and it did not stop, even in the midst having play dates. Many times when I couldn't get Anna calmed down, I would call Tammy just for support though the tears, so she was aware of what I was dealing with some nights. It was very nice because this particular night she offered to hold Anna while I left the house. I went out to sit on my porch swing, which had made the long move. We took turns holding her until all was calm.

Before the horrible thing, Michael Ray had been Anna's soccer coach for her little recreational soccer team and she had loved this. She really enjoyed her daddy taking her to her soccer games and watching her play. In an attempt for normalcy for her, I signed her up for Fall Soccer at the local park. We were assigned to a very gentle coach who worked very well with her though she was extremely apprehensive. When it came time for her to play her first game, I got her dressed in her little soccer uniform, her hair in pigtails just as she always had worn when she played soccer and drove out to the field. When we got there, she sat in the back seat and pronounced that she wasn't going out there unless her daddy was there. After thirty minutes and the game halfway through, I was able to get her out of the car and to the sidelines. She never actually played that game, but I decided that we would be content with small victories. I never actually asked for my children to be in such a state of transition so when crying spells would occur, I just tried to love them through it.

It was hard enough for me to express my feelings of the particular situation, much less for them to speak theirs. I am grateful to Anna's first grade teacher who saw, early on, Anna's gift of writing. She provided her with a journal called "Anna's Feelings Journal" in which Anna drew pictures and wrote captions under them. Many days, Anna wrote, "I am sad". As she learned to express her feelings, her crying nights began to subside.

Melody, on the other hand, always amazed me. She seemed to be a silent observer, however, when she needed to say something, she would tell me. She was good about saying she wanted to call her daddy or grandparents. I also think, even now, that she feels like she is my mother hen. If I were to ask her to make me a cup of coffee, it is her pleasure to do so. She knows that I need help and we have partnered well together. She also showed a lot of concern for Anna when Anna would have her crying spells. Melody, in some ways, probably had to grow up too soon due to the fact that many times, I have needed help therefore I have relied on her. She has made a good partner as she has learned how to cook, clip coupons, and find deals on beauty products as well as clothes. I know she has observed me handle finances and much to her father's dismay, she mentions the price of everything, much as I do; especially gas prices. He has mentioned to me before that he doesn't want them so focused on money, but honestly I think it is good to be cost conscious.

CHAPTER
TWENTY-TWO

August 22, 2011

Lord,

I come to you still as a broken mess. Will I ever be more than a big ball of confusion? I want so much to travel in the Light and put things where they need to be. Recovered is the word I choose for what I want. Right now, I feel tired weak and unhealthy. I feel like I can't put anything where it belongs in my head. I am having a very hard time managing right now.

Lord, I ask for peace. I need to be able to REST in You and rest physically. Of course I am drawn to be inconclusive with Michael Ray because now, he says he wants me back. You know, all the things I needed to hear a while back, he says now.

Jesus, I don't doubt that You are the healer of all things but I need to see fruit before I give any type of green light to that. Standing my ground in this area is so hard.

Lord, I am also struggling as a mother. I know I am trying to do the best and right things for them but I fail daily. I don't know what to do with Anna and how all this has affected her. It is evident that she has been forever changed.

Lord, I ask for more protection around my children. Lord, I ask that You would give them peace and comfort and that I would be enough that they can find peace and comfort in me.

I am in fear and worry that all that has taken place will cause my children eternal damage. They are my beautiful gifts and I pray over their hearts and lift them up to You.

Lord, I do ask for partnership. I don't enjoy being alone. I recognize I am at a scattered place where one minute I am struggling to be content with my surroundings and the other minute I hate everything about this life. When I ask for partnership, what I am really asking for is peace. Please be near me day in and day out. Fill up my cup and let it overflow with You.

I have been awake for over an hour and rambled plenty. Lord, please settle my heart. Calm Melody and Anna. Give us a good day in Your name.

Lord, we keep asking for something beautiful and better.

Giving you all the glory. Always.

Libby

During all of the transition, I needed to find a church. In all of my life, there was never a time where I did not attend a church service, and frankly, even today, I don't know how to do life without that weekly grounding. I had left South Fork Baptist Church due to my conflict with the pastor's beliefs on my horrible thing and what my future would be like if I ever remarried. I then had to leave the Bridge Community Church as well even though I loved them dearly due to proximity. I wanted to be a number. I didn't want to be a person with a proverbial scarlet letter on her chest, so in looking at all of the churches that were around, I decided to attend the biggest one of all. I can't remember how many services they had in hindsight but it was at least three or more on the weekend. I also learned that I enjoyed the rest that came with a Sunday morning, so I began driving a short distance on Saturday nights to what I would call a mega church. I liked that I could come in and be anonymous. I needed to be anonymous. With identity comes responsibility and I did not need any more than I already had on my plate.

The girls seemed to enjoy this time at the church and liked that they could pick attendance in the children's program or sitting with me in the sanctuary. There were three teachers that were having babies at the school and of course, in an attempt to be all in with co-workers, I knitted their babies little hats. I enjoyed this time that I could sit in the dark sanctuary after dropping my children off in childcare, be alone with my Jesus even if there were a thousand people in the room, sit quietly, and knit before the service started. Once again, knitting saved my day.

The principal that hired me at West was a sister in law to a gal that was in my class in high school, someone I fully intended on contacting. Before I could initiate that contact, I learned that her husband, also a classmate of mine, had passed away. It was all too soon. She was left to be a single mother of a very young son. My heart certainly went out to her. The entire town reached out to her. In no way is my situation or my horrible thing the same as hers, yet, I could somehow empathize parts of how the horrible thing in her own life was affecting her.

During this same time, I was retreating to the porch swing in the backyard of the shack just for some peace and clarity. Anna came out to join me. I remember that she aroused me from my thoughts and asked me how Jesus gets in your heart. I remember describing the love Christ showed us on the cross and how Jesus is the pardon for our sins. Her sweet mind and heart opened to the love of God and she made a decision to accept this in faith. In this moment, as I prayed for her on the porch swing, Anna began to settle.

We were still attending the large church in Louisville so the next time that we went I had Anna talk with a children's minister who listened to her heart. He offered to baptize her, however I knew it would be difficult with a divided family so we waited on it for a while. He said that even if she wasn't ready, she could still attend new believer classes. These classes met weekly for a period of time and I didn't feel that it would hurt anything for her to attend, so she did. They helped her understand the huge commitment she was making in life.

At the very same time that she began attending those classes, a ministry to single moms was brought up to me. Now, Tammy had always said that she didn't want to be the poster board for single moms and it seemed like it would be just that, an admittance of what we were if we attended the single mom classes, but the need was too deep and too great to be prideful about what I was so lost doing. I asked Tammy to attend with me so that I wouldn't be alone.

It was funny because the teaching team that I was on at school was trying to instill a college and career readiness mindset into the students, so as part of that initiative, they wanted us to adopt a state college and promote college readiness. As a staff, we were to wear this Murray State University shirt every Thursday, the same day that this class met, so every Thursday, I showed up wearing the same stupid t-shirt and jeans. There were three huge benefits to me being involved in this program. One, dinner was provided each week so I didn't have to cook for the children or me. Secondly, I really felt a strong sense of love and support from women that I didn't even know. This was very empowering. Lastly, they really helped me figure out how to stand on my own two feet financially. I was very scared that every move I was making was the wrong one and it was nice to have sound advice from wise people with no agenda of their own. We did this for about eight weeks and as helpful as it was, it was a blessing to be in it and then it was a blessing for it to be completed. It is extremely difficult for a single mom to work all day, load two kids up in the car and drive to another town for a meeting that would be getting over late and come home to try to do baths all before needing to start all over again the next day. I was only doing this with two children however Tammy was doing it with four. Overall, I believe the benefit of the class was greater than the hassle and I would certainly encourage others to take the class as well. Many nights when I was able to take the girls to childcare and retreat to the room where the dinner was, it was so nice just to sit in a semi quiet room and listen or if I was really tired just tune everything out.

You see, living in the one bedroom shack meant that I never had my own room to go to for alone time or peace. Part of God's design was for us to have this space together because we needed each other so much. As much as that was part of the divine plan, I still found that I needed my own space and time.

Another thing that happened that began to give me a little space was that my mom decided that she wanted to get my children on Wednesday nights and take them to her church for the Wednesday night supper and children's programs. This became another piece of sacred time in my life, a time where I could be alone with my thoughts. This also began my little addiction with quaint, individually owned coffee shops.

One morning, after I had dropped the girls off to school, I was on my way to Kroger to pick up something I needed for my own school day. As I was driving through the little town of Shelbyville, I saw a little coffee shop sign on the corner of Sixth and Main. I found a space on the side of the street and popped in. This was the beginning of a beautiful relationship between the sweet little shop, those that patron it and myself. Almost four years later, I can say without a doubt, it is like a little piece of home. When I need a safe haven, I can go there and just be. I've gotten to know each customer there as a friend. It really is like my own little version of Cheers. Literally, they do know me by name and I love them all so.

CHAPTER
TWENTY-THREE

It became time for Fall Break, a much-needed break from the path that I was paving for myself. My mom and my step-dad wanted to take the girls and me to Disney World. You truly do not say no to going to Disney when anyone offers. We spent a week in pure Disney Magic. It was a welcome vacation from the little shack from which we lived our busy little lives of adjustment.

I have three favorite moments from this trip. The first one was when we first got to the parks and they gave buttons to all who entered the park. Since this was my girls' first trip to Disney, they received a button that said "First Time Visitor". I had been before so I didn't want that button. I looked at the selection and picked out a button that had Cinderella on it and said, "Happily Ever After". The man said, "Ma'am, that button is for newlyweds who are on their honeymoon." I looked at him and said, "I know, but I still want the button." He looked puzzled for a moment and said, "Are you on your honeymoon?" to which I said, "No, I'm just here with my children." with a big smile on my face. That is when he got it. I didn't need a partner for a "Happily Ever After"... or maybe that's when it really resonated with me. Disney does a unique thing with those buttons. You are to wear them in the park and if you are a first timer, like my girls, the characters are to comment on your experience. Since I was wearing the button that said "Happily Ever After", I was repeatedly congratulated to which I replied "Thank you!" It was my inner victory. I felt that I did deserve to be thanked. One woman at a ride asked me where my husband was. I explained to her my inner victory. I was coming out of a divorce and I was going to be okay. She said, "Girl, I like the way you think. I'm going to get me one of those buttons too!" I hope she did.

The second memory I have was one night we had gone to Magic Kingdom with my step dad and Anna and I headed back over to the countries part of Epcot. This particular night, in the United States of America section of Epcot, Sugar Ray was in concert. I was already at Disney World with my favorite two kids in the entire world and bonus!!! Sugar Ray was in concert at the happiest place on Earth. I did what any good mom would do and bought my daughter and I the biggest turkey leg I could buy and a large coke to share and took my 6-year-old child to the front row where we ate our turkey leg and jammed with Sugar Ray.

The last memory I have of our trip to Disney made me mad at the time and now looking back, I can see the strength that was building in me mentally and physically. On our last night in the parks, the whole group, my mom, my stepdad, the girls and myself went to a night show at Hollywood Studios called *Fantasmic*. It was the most amazing night show that I had ever seen at Disney and I have seen several of their night shows over the years. Mickey was dressed as he was in Fantasia and fought off many of the Disney villains. After an amazing finale, it was time to make our way from the back of the park to the car. It was so very late and Anna-Kate had fallen asleep. I don't know why I even bothered looking around for help. It was up to me to carry her from the back of the park to the very front. It would be nice to find out what the distance in that was because if I were to guess, I would say it was at least a mile, if not more. I carried the dead weight of a six-year-old as far as I could and when I didn't think I could go any further, I did. At one point, I stopped and another parent took pity on me and offered their stroller for her to ride in for a while as their child was up and walking. I was able to push her to the gate of the park before I had to lift her from the stroller and keep walking to the car. It was so late at this point that the trolleys in the parking lots were finished running and we were left to walk another very long (seemed like another mile distance) to the car, I of course, was carrying Anna-Kate all the while. In that moment of carrying her, I was angry but also vindicated. I could take care of these little girls myself and nothing was going to keep me from it. I had many inner personal battles that I fought. Our time in Disney was a beautiful fulfilling time in which I grew and found rest and parts of myself. Oh, if only Fall Break, or any break for that matter could be longer. After a week of magic, we were back to our new daily grind.

CHAPTER
TWENTY-FOUR

A cherished author of mine, Angela Thomas, was scheduled to speak at the church I was attending and I really wanted to hear her. Of course, I talked Tammy into going with me to hear her: a speaker, writer and strong believer. I really don't remember everything that she said that day in her speech but I do remember the opportunity in which I was able to talk to her that night. After her speech, they had brought her to a room to sign books, yet the service wasn't complete. In an attempt to get past the masses that had come to hear her, I went on to the room and had almost the entire room to myself with her. Through tears, I told her about living with my children in the one bedroom shack and how my family was broken. She looked at me in love and said that when she was going through the very hardest times of her life a friend had said to her, "Sweetie, the Bible says we walk THROUGH the Valley of the Shadow of Death, we don't set up camp and live there." I knew what she meant. I knew I would get through. I knew that some days were hard, but I was getting stronger and healthier with each passing day. I smiled.

The holidays and winter were just around the corner and so was the time to search for a new home. I was beginning to make friends and find that people liked me. It's crazy. I had my identity wrapped up in "family" for so long, it was hard to try to figure out who I was apart from Michael Ray and the identity of being "Michael Ray's wife". I was beginning to add my maiden name back to my legal name just to have some sense of who I was and where I was rooted.

When the girls would go with their dad, I was beginning to have friends of my own who made sure that my social calendar was filled. Little did I know how much the placement at West Middle School would mean to me. I know I mentioned each of these gals before, but now I need to tell you in depth how much nothing is an accident with God. He had ready-made friends for me in this job.

All three of these women had significant roles in my first year at West. My schedule consisted of co-teaching a math class and two science classes as well as reading interventions taught by myself. I was assigned to use Sophie's room, so every day during third period, I would come in her room with my class and she would leave and go teach another class elsewhere. I'm not sure why at first they had me use her room and displace her, but that's how it is in education; it happens. Sophie and I got used to exchanging small conversations in passing back and forth from room to room and this is how we became friends.

Melissa, on the other hand, was my KTIP mentor. Since she was doing this, I was assigned to meet with her every so often and she was to observe my teaching and help me fill out many, many forms. Since it was my first year teaching and I had put so much on the line and move to Shelbyville, keeping a job for the next year was a must. Honestly, I never realized how hard a good teacher works and what it takes to try to do everything right. In teaching, you are never caught up. Even as I write this very sentence, I'm thinking of work I am sacrificing to get my story out. Everything seemed so urgent that first year and I was extremely overwhelmed with my personal trauma as much as I was trying to stay on my toes in a new job environment. Honestly, most days, those kids were lifesavers for me because for seven and a half hours a day, I thought about them rather than myself.

Melissa was there to help. On days I was overwhelmed, she calmed my fears. On days I completely freaked out about my observations, she would assure me that I was doing just fine. She too, was a single mother with two children that were her main responsibility. She was in the dating world and shared all of her stories with me, which helped me feel sane. It made me feel like someone else sought the same things I sought.

Many times, we would sit around her table at her house with a glass of wine and chat. She would invite Sophie over and I would soon learn of Sophie's divorce horror story as well. Sophie was the epitome of a sweet, dedicated southern wife. She had lived this life for almost thirty years when one day her world came crashing down. While Melissa was about a year and a half out of her divorce, Sophie was about a year out of hers and I was in the middle of mine.

When school was out for Melody and Anna, they had to ride the bus to West and wait for me to finish teaching before we could go home. Claire's daughter, Sarah, was also on that bus so they all got off at West together. They quickly became friends with Sarah and played with her in the classroom while waiting on their mothers to finish teaching. While Melody, Anna and Sarah were bonding, Claire and I began to bond as well. I learned that Claire came out of a very explosive situation and then her ex-husband remarried very quickly and moved to another state. Since he lives so far away, Claire has her children during the school year and then he has them during breaks. During the breaks when there is no daily grind, she doesn't get to enjoy them, she just must send them on to him. In essence, it is truly feast or famine with her and her children. I can't imagine how hard it would be as a teacher to finally make it to the day before Christmas break only to drive your children to the airport when you actually, finally had time to spend with them.

CHAPTER
TWENTY-FIVE

Early in November, Shelbyville does what Shelbyville does best; decorates for Christmas and lights up the town tree. My children were scheduled to be with their father for the weekend and for some reason, I desperately wanted to go to "Light Up Shelbyville". It would be the first time in years that I had been to a Shelbyville celebration. During one of our many KTIP talks, I must have roped Melissa into going with me to this event. I don't remember all of the circumstances, but we somehow ended up together for the night walking around the streets of Shelbyville, standing in front of the courthouse for the countdown of the lighting of the town tree and even posing for a photographer with little elf hats on our heads. We were so very cute. I remember being very humbled at Melissa's few tears that were shed as the tree was lit, because in the silence of our hearts, we both knew that this was a moment for families and yet, here we stood somewhat displaced, but with each other. We had two more stops to make that night as we went to the movie store to pick up Hope Floats and the liquor store for some wine. We were all set for a cheesy girl's night in after freezing our tails off at the lighting of the town tree and the samplings of pumpkin fudge.

It was close to Thanksgiving and I had decided for the month of November, I would make a public statement via social networking of one thing that I was thankful for per day. The single mom class was ending and I was looking for an apartment or house to rent. My house still had not sold in Hodgenville and I had started the process in terms of talking with the mortgage company about something called Deed in Lieu of Foreclosure because if I was going to try to move out of the shack into a rightful place of space for my girls, I couldn't keep making a house payment on a house we were not living in. It was beginning to get very cold in the shack and the divorce process was moving slowly. I knew that I wanted the girls for Christmas. In my mind, I could not bear spending Christmas without them, so I proposed that Michael Ray would have them for Thanksgiving. He did not seem to have an issue with that so, I spent Thanksgiving with my family and the girls spent Thanksgiving with him and his family. It was still hard not seeing my in-laws on a holiday I was used to spending with them, but I made it through. My sister began to be a big help to me during those family occasions where she knew I was lost without the girls. Tammy always had her door open on weekends and holidays where I would become lost. Little by little my life was taking shape in a whole new way that I didn't even believe was possible a year earlier.

November 20, 2011

Dear Jesus,

You are so amazing to me. I read from Revelation and I know and understand that the true meaning of the book is that You want us to have our own personal revelation about You; about who You are, who You were and what is to come. Thank You for sharing your revelations with us as we are your creation and mere mortals in Your ultimate design. The process of reading Your word in the New Testament has been a reward for me. It has reiterated truths I already knew about You and your love for us even though we as humans do everything we can to try to change how You love us and put conditions on that love. You love us with blind incomprehensible love and your directives to us are for our benefit and the glory of Your kingdom.

Lord, daily, moment by moment, I am in awe of You. Your provisions for my heart and me are amazing. Thank You for being a Father to me. At this time, thank You for showing me my new normal. Thank You for helping me do the job of a mother that is set out before me. Things have changed for me in most every way I know of in a year's time all except for You Jesus. You have been the same.

Be with me in the coming days. I don't know how I will respond. Help me to be mindful of my children and their hearts during this time.

In Your Precious Name,

Libby

The anniversary of the horrible thing was quickly approaching. Anniversaries of horrific events can always be a little scary. PTSD is real for a reason. I didn't experience a lot of major trauma but I did have some anxiety as the anniversary and Thanksgiving were approaching. I put in as many safety nets I could as possible. I made sure I had friends on hand that I could talk to and plans for the days surrounding the anniversary to keep my mind off the events at hand. Somehow, I came across this particular quote during this time that empowered me and gave me strength. It simply stated: "Be careful that a moment of madness in a tough season doesn't affect a lifetime of possibilities. Seasons change!" I just found this to be very good advice for myself. I don't know who said it, but I clung to it during this time. I loved the part that said possibilities. Possibility with a capital P; that is what I needed in my life. Like I said, I was beginning to walk on my own and not be completely afraid. I was building confidence in my own decision-making. I was growing as a teacher in the classroom and I was getting healthier.

The memories of sharing a little one bedroom apartment with my two girls and cooking on a hotplate are sweet and something that I will always remember doing with them, but we were all three ready for a home that had a little more space for each person. We wanted a place where I could pull out all of our belongings that had sat in storage for six months. I began the process of looking for a rental property since I still owned the house in Hodgenville and the negotiations on that house were moving very slowly.

My family and I celebrated Thanksgiving together and then I went to Tammy's to be safe from the day. Thankfulness was full in my heart, as I had survived the worst year of my entire life. I am eternally grateful to the people that were in my life and made it possible for me to thrive when many times I wanted to crawl into hole and never come out. My friends were not about to let that happen.

CHAPTER TWENTY-SIX

After many considerations of a single-mom budget and looking at several places, I ended up choosing a sweet little town house. It was fifteen hundred square feet, had an upstairs and downstairs, columns in the living area, large bedrooms and a functional kitchen. It was exactly what I was looking for at the right price. I began making the necessary financial arrangements for the move.

Since I had my group of girlfriends that I was quickly learning was a gift, I decided that I wanted to do something special for them. I knew that the holidays would be hard for me due to all of my new circumstances and so I figured that they were for them as well. The day that school got out, Tammy let me plan a holiday dinner at her house so that I could invite my new friends, show them some love and appreciation. I made it an Italian night, asked everyone to bring a salad or bread and those of us who could be there, sat, laughed, chatted and enjoyed each other's company at a time where we were so used to having the company of our families from Christmases of the past.

This particular dinner also happened to fall on the weekend anniversary of my wedding to Michael Ray. I didn't know how I would handle the twelfth anniversary of my wedding since all meaning that came with my vows was null and void at the time. I was aware of the day, but tried to ignore it. I didn't talk about it and I didn't talk to Michael Ray on that day. By treating it as if it were just seven days before Christmas and not anything else, it was easier.

Christmas was coming quickly and I was trying to figure out how to celebrate with the girls in the shack while preparing to move. I did not have room for a big tree or decorations. We actually spent the night with my parents at their house on Christmas Eve and that is where Santa Claus visited the children that year. My friend Michelle, from Hodgenville, loaned me a little pink Christmas tree to display for the girls in the shack. They loved hanging the little ornaments painted with Disney princesses onto the tree. The little tree was perfect; however, we never could get the lights to work.

December 22, 2011
Lord,

What a Christmas Season this has been already. Me, Melody and Anna in our little shack with our pink Christmas tree with the lights that don't work. Lord, I pray that they look back on this time and realize that I have tried so hard for them and I pray that they are beginning to have special memories of a new time in our lives. I have started new traditions in gift making and cookie decorating. I want them to have good memories in the face of adversity at all times. Yes, I am seeing that, though my family was severed, we are a family just the same. Me and Melody and Anna. Yes, I love them, even when they scream and they scream a lot.

Lord, I am constantly saying, thank You for Your beautiful provision over me. You have provided friends when I needed them. You have opened doors that needed to be opened and closed doors that needed to be shut. That I can have an intimate conversation with the Creator of the Universe who still tends to the nano billions of things beyond me is amazing.

The Baby in a manger, Your Son, is what Christmas is all about, not me. If we ever make it something more than eternal love and sacrifice, we have ruined the true meaning of Christmas. Happy Birthday Jesus. I love You.

Love,
Libby

Michael Ray and I had talked and it was decided that I would bring the children to him after my family celebrated all of our Christmas Eve and Christmas morning festivities. Since this was my first Christmas without my beloved in-laws, I agreed and even offered to drive the children to his Mamaw's house. Since I had been so strong and successful at Thanksgiving, I thought that I would be able to make it through Christmas. After having my girls all to myself for Christmas, I loaded them into my car and set out for Leitchfield. I thought that I was strong; however, I was not this day. Driving into that old familiar driveway, walking into the family that I had known and loved for so long was too much. Emotions flooded in my heart. I smiled and cried at the same time. I had thought that I would be able to stay and chat for a while, maybe drink some of Mamaw's Christmas Punch, but I could not. I knew I was welcome, but I simply could not do it. The grief became too much to bare all at once. The wounds that I was confident were healing burst open and my heart gushed with brokenness and loss. I ran out to the front porch so I didn't make a scene and make their Christmas about me. Michael Ray came out to check on me and in the quiet moment, I appreciated the fact that he understood the loss that I was feeling.

I got in my car and tears unleashed. I cried for myself. I cried for my children and I hurt that my Christmas days were never going to be the same. My cousin Laura had sent out a Facebook invitation for an open house at her home on Christmas Day. I decided that, rather than being alone, I should definitely visit. I called her between breaths and told her I was on my way.

Remember, Laura and I had never been very close, but her role in this past year was key in my life. My face was a puffed up, blurry mess as I pulled into her driveway. I was welcomed into their home with open arms. Laura, sensitive to my needs at that time, asked me if I wanted to look at their book collection. Of course, I did, but in hindsight, it was really code for "Joey, why don't you go work your magic with Libby?" Joey was a hospital chaplain and had a very calming demeanor. It was just what I needed that day. We looked at his books on behavioral theories and theologies and he showed me his sword collection. By the time we rejoined the family, I was ready for a tough game of Scrabble and those Ritz cracker things covered in white chocolate. At the end of the day, I ended up at Tammy's house for the night. There is still something to be said about snuggling up on flannel sheets in a king size bed in the comfort of the love and protection of a good friend. The true meaning of Christmas was not lost. At the end of the day, it was still about a Baby in a manger that came to save the world from ourselves and I could rest in that after all, the next day was a very big day.

The big moving day was the day after Christmas. I had two male co-workers (more wonderful people from West) who gave me their day and time to help me move into my new little townhouse. Moving day was cold and slushy, however we moved forward. During the middle of the third or fourth load, my friend Mannie looked at me and said, "Libby, you live in perfection!" I looked at him puzzled and he said, "Yeah, you live in the seventh building, number seventy-seven!" I liked that. It felt good that things were looking up enough to live in "perfection".

After all things had been moved and put into the townhouse, Mannie and Matt went on their way. I was left alone in my new home with all of my belongings, many of which had been packed up since July. I was too tired to even try to figure out what to do next with the boxes and all of the stuff...I just decided to get in bed. I walked up the stairs into the bedroom and surveyed the room. All of the furniture had been placed in the room, however, there was no semblance of any order. The bed was in the middle of the room. I was so glad to see this bed as it had been in storage since July and Anna and I had been sleeping on the bed that was in the shack, (which was on an uneven floor so I had slept tilted downward for six months). I looked around and found some blankets. I laid one on the mattress and crawled up on top of it. I then pulled the other blanket up over me and fell asleep for ten hours straight. I was exhausted. If you know me at all, you know I really can't sleep past seven in the morning, so it was an odd occurrence for me to sleep until nine o'clock. School started in a week so I had one week's worth of time to make my new space livable. I still had a few minor trips to make to pick some things up from the shack.

The next few days were filled with visitors stopping by to help do some unpacking and rearranging. I felt so loved and supported as

I made the moves that needed to be made to make the space. It was wonderful to have my things around me. Now, I of all people, will be the first to tell you that things don't matter, but it was nice on these cold January days to have familiar items nearby. I worked very hard trying to make the townhouse a home that the girls would be happy to live in and be excited about. I spent hours working in their room, lovingly placing each toy that they had forsaken for sixth months in a special spot. You see, I had only let them pick about four toys each to have at the shack, because there was no room. In this new place, even though they were sharing a room, there was room for each toy to have its own space. Claire came over with a housewarming gift of fresh flowers and helped me put the living room together. Melissa and Tammy also helped with what they could. My dad came all the way to my townhouse to help me set up the washer and dryer and my mom came by. Everyone was so happy for me to have a place of my own.

One day, while I was moving a few things in, I had the door open and when I came back into the living room to shut the door, there was a man at my door. He was older, with a nice smile, cowboy boots and a big belt buckle. In talking with him for just a few minutes, I learned that he only lived in the townhouse on the other end of the building on a part-time basis as he traveled half the year to judge in horseshows. He was very big in the horse industry and traveled all over the United States judging horse shows. I soon found out that he was a divorcée and had taken a little bit of sympathy out on me for my situation. I also found out that he was good with a screwdriver. He was very happy to learn that I had two daughters who would be home the night of New Year's Eve. Since we have lived in our little townhouse, he has treated my girls like a second set of grandchildren.

CHAPTER
TWENTY-SEVEN

New Year's Eve came faster than I could blink since I had spent a week of non-stop packing and organizing. The girls were to come home in the early evening. I had a fun night planned of staying in our home and playing board games. When they arrived, they were so excited and toured themselves through every nook and cranny of the new place, noticing where I had put this or remembering that! They were so overjoyed to see their new toys. I felt so good and so alive, finally having the place of my own. It was a little sad waiting for my divorce to be finalized after the New Year. I would have loved to start the New Year with a clean slate, but I was quickly learning that God's plan is always better. It would be just a few more months before that became a thing of the past. Most of the ramifications of the horrible thing had settled. The girls and I played Clue, Monopoly and Life. We had no cable hooked up yet so we ended up watching the ball drop live from the tiny screen of my smart phone. As the girls and I all piled in my big bed together in my new room, I couldn't have been happier with where 2011 had taken us. I looked forward to where 2012 was going to go.

Tammy had acquired or stumbled across a book that we enjoyed reading from time to time. I believe it was called Six Word Memoirs. Some of them were funny. Some were very real. The one that I remember sticking out was "I can see red flags sooner." That six word sentence has a lot of meaning. I decided that at the end of the year I would write my own six word memoir which is not anything like all the words of this story, but yet, I feel, in some ways, it conveys the same meaning. My memoir for the year of 2011 was simply, "I never gave up, I'm okay." And it was so.

In the days to come, the girls and I enjoyed quicker rides to school, faster rides home at night and the freedom we had when we wanted to find some space or solitude of our own. My confidence was soaring and my weight was dropping.

January 15, 2012

Dear Jesus,

I come to You again, still here, as my messed up self. So many things I am settled about and yet, so much more that I am completely restless over. I love my new place and I am so thankful to have it. It is the perfect size and style for me. I know those are just superficial and so many people have so much less than me, so please help me find ways to use my resources to help others.

I am starting to get a grip on my job. Thank You for providing awesome people to work with and to help me in my move. Thank You for showing me a way that men can be rather than how I have experienced them to be.

Thank You for meeting all my needs as You have. You always shown Yourself and protect me at just the right time. Lord, I feel like You are finally giving me rest. A resting time is what I have longed for.

Although I am still unsettled about things, I feel as though I am coming to an end. Just to put pen to paper, some of the things I am unsettled about are...

The house in Hodgenville and what to do...I can't keep making house payments on it and provide for my girls here. My sinus problems, the Speech Team at Shelby West, finalizing the divorce, new relationships with men, Michael Ray's job opportunities, any angst I have over the future...

Lord, I place all these fears that creep into my life and my sleep and place them at Your feet. You amaze me, God, that you would care about how I feel in the midst of all that must encompass You.

One thing I have been reflecting upon today God, is my consideration of relationships with men in the future. I want to write down what I think I will be looking for so it can be a tangible list to keep.

*Believer in You

*Can talk with me about anything

*Giving of time and resources/financially responsible

*Not judgmental or critical of others

*Likes to read

* Healthy sexually (no baggage or past issues)

*Professional

*Good Health

Lord, if I find someone who is likeminded in these areas, I don't care what he looks like. I am always attracted to intellect and emotional connections anyhow. I would like him to have at least five of the areas I have laid out. The deal breaker is not a genuine faith in You. I can accept any combo of these seven aspects. I just think it is important for me to have any scales removed from my eyes so that I am not blinded by something that appears to be right but is wrong.

Lord, I know You have a plan for me so I really leave things up to You as to how they play out. I will just be an active participant after Your own heart. Let me say Your words and walk where Your feet walk. Let me be Your hands. Open my eyes to things that I need to see and my mind and heart to what I need to know.

Amen,
Libby

Writing this presently in 2015, I look back on this one particular prayer and I wonder if I was premature in my thinking about men, and relationships. I have several thoughts on that topic. One, God created me to be who I am and this is obviously something I desired so I am glad that I went on and spoke it rather than suppressed my feelings. Just because I was hurt by a relationship doesn't mean that I didn't desire one with the possibility of real true love to be a part of my life. I thought that it was important to look over what I felt would work in my life and be specific to myself and the men that I might come in contact with.

I was getting healthier and physically and mentally stronger still. I was beginning to be the butterfly that was breaking free from the cocoon. Metamorphosis is truly a process. I have always maintained that, after what happened to me, I am more like a butterfly with a broken wing. There is always going to be a scar there of what happened no matter how much I want certain parts of my life to be pure. There are daily reminders of what that life was and how far I was from it.

As I was becoming healthier, men were beginning to notice this single chick running around town. While I liked the attention some, it really was new to me as I was not even fully divorced and hadn't been on the dating scene since before cell phones or internet. I was paying attention to this attention enough to get my big toe wet and get out in the water.

On this journey that I was on, there were times that I would completely panic about many of the miniscule things that I listed in my last prayer I shared with you. I was continuously reading through scripture, as one of my goals was to read the Bible in its entirety. One of the verses that stuck out to me and gave me hope in the winter of 2012 was Jude 1:2 (The Message) which says: "Relax, everything's going to be all right; rest, everything's coming together; open your hearts, love is on the way!" These little verses would come to me right before or after a breaking point usually and they would be just the manna that I needed to keep myself going. Proverbs 16:19 is another verse that makes its way to me repeatedly in life. "We plan the way we want to live, but only God makes us able to live it." I knew then and know now that apart from Jesus and His way I am nothing.

In the beginning of January 2012, I found that I really enjoyed using a full kitchen again and making my girls many homemade meals. On the cold nights after work, I would come home with the girls, put on pajamas and make dinner. Once I helped them with homework, I would peruse Pinterest, which became one of my small wintertime addictions. I loved looking up recipes and craft ideas, tagging them with the full intent of completing the project on a snow day. We didn't have too many snow days that winter, but just enough to enjoy a day off here and there.

March 4, 2012

Dear Jesus,

Thank You for making me and giving me this life and all of my senses. I can feel the cold dampness of my just washed hair against my neck and enjoy seeing the sunrays peek through the curtains on the window. Even the slight headache I have is fine with me.

Lord, help me to love people as You would. That is all I want to do. Please give me focus as I move forward in this life- alone or with someone by my side. Please have it be whom You would desire for my life. You – who knows me and created me. Thank You that I am told that I am "doing it". I need that conformation quite often. I need to hear that, in the wake of this horrible thing, I survived. I am okay. I do need purpose and I am unsure of what the purpose is at this time.

Lord, I know I have already written plenty just about me but I am so depleted and empty sometimes, I just need You to fill me up. Lord, let me shine, not because I need credit but because you created me with a need to shine bright. Lord, help me financially take care of all of the business related aspects of my life. Thank You for always meeting my needs. Help me to have self-control where self-control is limited. It's funny how I waited for the perfect job and You unrolled the carpet just when I needed You to. Now I am waiting again... waiting for what, I'm not sure, just waiting. Help me to see purpose in it all. Help me to take care of my girls the best way possible.

Lord, as always, I lift them up to You. Thank You for Melody's Odyssey of the Mind group and the fact that Anna has found a place with friends as well. Thank You that they are happy. I need to see that for them. I want to know that I am making their life better and teaching them. Thank You for your love, care, direction and attention to everything but most of all, for Melody Grace and Anna-Kate.

Love,

Libby

127

Libby Sears Blair

Chapter
Twenty-Eight

My relationships with others in Shelby County were growing and being reignited after being gone all those years. One thing I love about Shelbyville is that you can never truly leave it. The town is so friendly and embraces you and your current season of life. My girlfriends at work and I were strengthening our bond as well. One day in the hustle and bustle of middle school, Sophie said to me, "Hey, let's go to Florida over Spring Break!" The idea sounded so foreign to me. I felt like I needed to go home and discuss it with someone, but who? It really was just okay for me to say, "Sure!" Later in the week, Melissa and I were meeting about KTIP stuff and completely off task; I mentioned that Sophie and I were going to Florida over Spring Break. She blurted out that she wanted to go too. I checked with Sophie and she was thrilled! The more the merrier. So, we had plans for a trip to Barefoot Bay. We immediately named ourselves the Barefoot Baywatch Babes, because, you know, we were! We definitely had something to look forward to. In the meantime, I occupied my time reading books, writing in my prayer journals and, of course, focusing on my two precious baby girls. It was nice to let life somewhat develop and shape itself without heavy decision making though I was awaiting some things to come through in writing which would end the frustrations of owning a property and living elsewhere and the fact that my divorce would be final in the near future.

Now, if you will remember, my car wasn't the most reliable vehicle in other stories I've shared. I already knew it was on its last leg, I just didn't know how long the last leg would last and so it is with paid off vehicles. I was hoping to get a few more miles out of it before facing the problem of buying a new car, however, my car and I did not have the same idea. It was having all kinds of issues and one of the sweet ladies at work who had taken me under her wing insisted that I go see her husband who had an auto mechanic shop. I am not one who claims to know anything about cars. All I knew was that something wasn't running right. I was off on this particular day because I had made Anna a doctor's appointment for a check-up. After having her checked out, I decided I had enough time before Melody was to get out of school to have my car checked out. I took it to Eddie in Louisville and he looked it over for me. I was glad to go there because I knew I could trust him. Of course, the diagnosis was not good. He recommended not driving it out of Shelbyville, which was not good because I wasn't even in Shelbyville at the time that he told me that. As I started off toward home, about five miles away from the auto shop, the car stopped. When I say that the car stopped, it really did stop forever, right in the middle of a very busy US 60. Luckily, it wasn't rush hour and I was able to get it moved off the road fairly quickly. (It was times like these when I felt truly helpless as a single woman who was used to having a husband to call upon when a car broke down.) All I knew to do was to call AAA and wait for them to come get the car and me. Poor Anna was sitting patiently in the backseat as this interaction went down. The thing I have never liked about AAA is the fact that when they come to tow your car, if you need a ride, you have to get in the car with the man that you don't know. This was the case on this particular day. I was fortunate that he didn't have to take us very far back to the auto repair place because we hadn't made it that far home yet. When Eddie went back out to look at the car again, for the second time that day, he confirmed the death of my little car. Great, now what to do? Here I was in Louisville, Kentucky in the middle of the workday with my daughter and no way to get home.

As I have said, one thing that was very difficult for me that first year was recognizing that it is okay and necessary to ask for help. I certainly needed help that day. Thank God for cell phones and text messaging as I began to send out SOS signals to the girls at West. Melissa agreed to get Melody from school and Angela, Eddie's wife volunteered to drive all the way to Louisville after work to get me. Anna and I had few hours that we needed to burn. Providentially, for us, across the large four lane highway that is US 60 was a Jason's Deli. I have never thought it was a good idea for pedestrians to cross a huge road like that especially with a six year old in tow, but off we went. For some reason, the memory of the dead garter snake I saw on the highway on that day has always stuck out in my mind. I just found it weird that as I was crossing a four-lane road with my baby girl in the middle of a March day, I would see a dead snake. After we had eaten at the deli, we sat at a table where Anna watched me devise a plan. I needed a car, immediately. Suddenly, I was faced with a grown up decision that I had to make without help, without partnership. It was a very scary thought. Though I didn't want Michael Ray to be a part of my decision-making, I knew he needed to be a part of the plan. I called him and basically demanded that he drive to my house the next morning so that he could watch Anna who had a doctor's note to be out of school and let me drive his car to the car shop. Let me explain why I included him in this particular situation. I needed to obtain a vehicle quickly to be able to transport our children around and so I felt it important for him to be part of the solution.

Now, I am normally one to research consumer reports before buying something big. I usually know what I want months in advance, plan and save for it, while trying to decide which retail store will get my business, I was taught to do this by my grandmother. I learned so much when I got to see her daily while living in Campbellsville and going to college. She helped me buy all of my college books. We would research the best place to buy the book for the cheapest price. When she stopped driving and going to the grocery herself, she would have me to go to the grocery for her. I would always be armed with the Kroger circular circled with the deals she wanted as well as any coupons she had clipped. At the time, I just thought her frugal living was a sign of her childhood in the depression. I now know, it was just good common sense. She taught me so much, yet I paid attention so little. I just thought I would always be able to rely on her, that when I had a financial question she would always be there. Now, here I was getting ready to buy a car on my own. I wasn't doing it because I wanted to. I was doing it because I had to and Grandma's mind was slipping. She wasn't able to help me.

The next morning Michael Ray arrived and handed over the car keys. As I left, he had settled with Anna on the couch. Tammy drove a Toyota Pathfinder so my first stop was to go to the Toyota dealership because when in doubt, I did the things that worked for Tammy. I had an idea of what kind of vehicle I thought I would like. I always thought that the mini SUV's were cute and functional for a mom, so I set out to look at them. There was a really nice SUV that was a hunter green color with tan leather interior. I don't remember what it was called but I remember how sharp it was. I parked Michael Ray's car in a spot and walked over to look at it. A salesman came over to me immediately. I remember that he kind of gave me the creeps. His wide smile revealed his gold tooth. He had slicked back hair and he touched me on the shoulder. He asked me if I would like to have that car. After shaking his hand off of my shoulder, I tried, very nonchalantly, to say it was okay. I did not want to give this man an inch until I found out more about the vehicle. Within minutes, he worked his uncanny car sales magic and had photocopied my driver's license and handed me the keys for a test drive. I asked if I could have it for a while and they seemed okay with that. I found it odd how easy it was to test-drive a vehicle. I drove it to a diner to grab a bite to eat and think. While there, I whipped out my phone and sent out a Facebook message asking for friends to give their suggestions on car dealerships. I needed all the help I could get and it was good to solicit the opinions of the masses. There was a retired teacher who substituted at West very frequently, whom I had befriended on Facebook. She sent me a message to go to a Ford dealership to speak with her boyfriend. I drove the little green thing over to the Ford dealership. It was kind of funny because as soon as I pulled up, all of the young car salesmen began to tell me that I needed a Ford, not a Toyota. Seeing how I was a little nervous about talking to salesmen, I was happy to say I was there to see Larry. I guess they realized that I was there to see a "big dog" and they backed down quite easily. I trusted Jenna and felt that she wouldn't steer me wrong. Instead of trying to talk to me about vehicles, I was happy because he talked to me about what I was really concerned with, which was money. Once we had all of the money figured out, he sent me out to the lot with a young man that he had handpicked for me. I was drawn to the SUV's once again. We test-drove a Ford Escape. They began asking me what color I liked and what kind of interior I wanted. In my head, I still really liked the little green thing. I couldn't decide between the two. I told them I needed to think about it. I then took the little green SUV back to Toyota and asked them to give me a price. I grew suspicious because they kept talking about payments, but would not tell me the price on the vehicle. I finally left to go home to see the girls. On my way to the girls, I was almost in tears. I had not been prepared to have to make a decision like this so quickly. I was scared. I was stubborn. I didn't want to do it. I desperately wanted the advice of my grandmother who was not able to tell me anything. I kept thinking…What would Grandma do? Well, whenever Grandma had trouble making a decision, she would call her brother Dick, my cousin Laura's father. The best thing that I knew to do was to call Laura. I was in tears when I told her that I wished that I could talk to my Grandma. She was very good at giving me the direct advice that I needed that day. She said, "When your grandfather died, Betty didn't have a driver's license, but she got out there and learned how to drive." Then she said, "Libby, what is going to happen if you don't buy a car today?" I thought about it and in laughter through tears, I said, "I won't have a car." "Exactly", she said, "So, you have to buy a car today." And I knew she was right. It was a matter of me stepping completely outside of my comfort zone and deciding between the two vehicles and doing it. I already had Ford telling me I was approved, I just didn't have Toyota telling me that, though I sort of liked their vehicle better.

I took the girls and went back to Toyota and tried one last time to find out about the price of the vehicle. I guess the weird guy figured out that I was serious and this time he took me to a table. He began mumbling about how nice my nails were. He asked me if I knew that their oil change service included free manicures for women while you waited. They still didn't tell me the price of the SUV. Once again I asked about the price and this time, he took a piece of paper out and hand wrote, "I will buy the car if we can agree on the payments" and then drew a line and an x beside it for me to sign my name. I looked at it and became very irritated. I was tired of playing with him. I told him that he had five minutes to get me the actual price of the car not a payment. He said, "Why? So you can compare to Ford or somewhere else?" Uh yeah, exactly, I thought in my head. I looked at him, in front of my girls and said, "It's called consumerism!" He got up and went to find his manager. While he was gone, I texted Larry from Ford and asked if they had the Escape in Steel Blue. I got back a response of yes. Right then and there, my mind was made up. We went to the parking lot and got in Michael Ray's car. I looked up and saw my creepy sales guy running out to me with his manager in tow. He was yelling "Wait, wait! I have a price." I told them I was sorry, I needed to go and little Anna who had been so patient through all of this yelled out of the back seat-"It's called CONSUMERISM!" in her snarky little girl voice. Oh, they really do pay attention to everything that we do. At Ford, all I had to do was sign for the vehicle. They handed me the keys and I was suddenly driving a brand new vehicle that had twelve miles on it.

It was my very own car, a vehicle that I had picked out on my own. I felt a little proud during this moment. I was worried about the payments but happy nonetheless to have something new and a safe vehicle to drive my two girls to and fro. The vehicle had a Sync sound system in it. It's basically hands free driving. They showed me how to use it at the dealership and on the way home; I received a phone call from the mortgage company. The deal that I had worked out on the house was complete. The moment I needed my funds available to make the car payment, the money was freed up from the mortgage company on a house that I didn't even live in anymore. This was Providence.

The next day, I went to work without any qualms, just happy to drive my little vehicle. The girls loved that it was called an Escape. I kind of liked that too. There is a lot of freedom in the word Escape. It is not like I was going to run away physically, but getting in my Escape for a mental escape while driving with windows down and music blaring was very welcoming. I also enjoyed the little moon roof that was in the roof of the vehicle.

The last day of the week, I got the girls up as usual and when I went out to the car, I opened the door to at least two inches of rain in the vehicle. I was not used to the little moon roof that I was learning to enjoy so much. It had been a beautiful day the day before, and I had been enjoying the sun shining down on my shoulders as I drove. Now, the car was soaking wet. The brand-new car had water all over it and what was worse was my bag of papers was soaked.

Anyone who knows me knows that I rarely carry a purse, but I usually, almost, always have a bag in my car filled with papers. Those papers can range from the latest utility bill to a personal journal. Most all of the papers that I carry with me require a personal response. The idea is that if I ever have extra time (yeah, right), I can tackle what is in the bag. The contents of the bag at this time had enormous personal value to me. There were all of the papers regarding the purchase of the vehicle, there were my pending divorce papers, all of my financial documents from which I was trying to form a budget around and a few uplifting cards from friends to keep me going. At this time, this bag was an extension of my life and everything I was going through. Horrified, I looked in the car at the water. The cup holders were each holding about two inches of water. How could I have done such a thing? My new vehicle only had about fifty miles on it. Knowing we had to get to school, I quickly sucked it up, ran in the house and grabbed some beach towels for us to sit on as we drove in to school. My girls, my two sidekicks who watch my reaction to everything, sat quietly in the car, as they knew I was overwhelmed. I dropped them off to their elementary school and went onto work. I had had exactly one day to be proud of the purchase before this. When I walked into work, Sophie was standing there with a big smile on her face. "How do you like the new car?" she said. I began to cry. I hadn't really just sobbed like this in a while, but I guess the stress of buying a new vehicle under the time constraints, the house situation being fully complete, having to involve Michael Ray in my situation, knowing the finalization of my divorce was pending, as well as every paper that was attached to my life being completely drenched was too much. No students were in the hallways yet, and as people noticed my tears, they began to come over and console me. Angela called her husband to see what I needed to do to get the water out of the car. Sophie took charge, took my wet bag to her classroom, and laid every paper I had in that bag out to dry. If anyone who wanted to be nosey had walked into that room that day, they could have seen every aspect of my life drying in a middle school classroom. To this day my legal papers surrounding the divorce are still a little wavy and ruffled.

I was learning that I had this capability to get back up pretty quick after being knocked down. After school, the Escape was not as wet as it was that morning. I had been advised to use a shop vac and baking soda to get the water out. It worked. My papers were dry and I was beginning to rest for the weekend.

CHAPTER
TWENTY-NINE

At some point between March and April, I received the final word. The judge had signed my papers and all of the vows we had said had no meaning. I'm glad I don't remember the date because dates tend to haunt me. The less I remember about *when* something happened, the less likely I am to notice it again the following year. I only want good things to be full circle events that I can celebrate. I guess, whatever day it was, when I pulled the envelope out of the mailbox, I knew what I was holding. It was the official end. I laid the papers on the dashboard and ignored them. I went on in the house and did dinner, homework, baths and bedtime. I called Tammy on the phone to tell her they had arrived. We talked for a while and then I went to bed. That weekend, the girls and I ended up at her house, where they played with her children and I sat on the porch swing outside with Tammy on her deck. I poured myself a glass of wine and in the presence of a good friend; I opened the envelope. It was just a paper. It had my name and his on it, just like the marriage certificate. It was over. I looked at it for a while. She looked at me look at it. Tears came for a moment and then they left just as fast. The permanent damage had already been done way before the papers arrived. I really had loved him and given him what I could and it was all over now. Officially over. I placed the papers back in the envelope. When I came home, I filed them away and to this day; there has not been a reason to look at them again.

The little coffee shop was a safe haven for me and still is. I can go there and just be. There was a particular guy who often frequented it when he was off work, so we had made friends. One particular Saturday, a weekend I didn't have the girls, I was sitting in the back where the regulars sit, knitting a scarf and chatting with him. We discussed a movie we both had interest in seeing and he asked if I wanted to go that night. Oddly enough, I was not clued into the fact that he was interested in me or that this might have been a "date". I said sure and went home to get a warmer jacket. I said that I would meet him back at the shop. At home, I looked in the mirror; I had not been wearing any makeup that day. I wondered if I should put makeup on, and for whatever reason, I decided not to. Yes, I went on my first post-divorce date with no makeup, a ponytail and converse tennis shoes. The movie wasn't good but the conversation was. About an hour into our time together, I realized that he considered this a date. Then I began to panic. I hadn't been on a date since 1998. The inner dialogue in my head ran rapid. I tried to focus, but I couldn't. I quickly began to withdraw and put protectors up. I wasn't ready for dating but here, clueless me, found myself on a date. It wasn't horrible at all. He was very nice and I think he understood how new I was to everything. After our evening, I heard from him sporadically, which was fine. I appreciated his interest in me however I didn't know what to do with it at the time.

Another new thing for me was that I began visiting a new church. The mega church was good for what it was, however, I was beginning to insert myself more into the community and I needed a connection. I didn't feel comfortable at the church that my parents went to, maybe because mom had placed me on the prayer list and I didn't want to feel like a victim. Also, it had changed so much from the church that I grew up in. When I looked around, it did not seem comfortable or familiar. I thought about all that I knew about churches and what I knew about God and where He was meeting me in my journey and considered the possibilities of a place where I could have more of a connection than I was finding at the big church. I have a friend; one I mentioned that I saw over the summer of my separation that had a large part in this decision. We have known each other for years and have always been the kind of friends that do not remain close perpetually, but drift in and out of each other's lives. He had grown up a Presbyterian. (Now, I am hesitant to bring up denominations for a long period in this book, because I believe we are all God's people, I was just looking for what would work best for me.) He always had such an openness and care for others, something I was drawn to in him and something I desired for my own life. I decided something must have fostered those values in him and sought it out. Another friend of mine, Brandy had also grown up in this church. In fact, her mother had offered to keep my children once a week while I was at faculty meetings. One wintry Sunday morning earlier in the year, my water heater had broken and I needed a shower. I knew I could call them and they would offer me the use of their bathroom. After showering there, Gary asked me if I might want to go to church with them sometime. At the time, I said no, but I began to consider the little Presbyterian Church on the corner of Seventh and Main.

CHAPTER
THIRTY

Spring break was upon us and I was really getting a chance to spread my wings and fly. This would be my first big trip without a family member since college. I was so excited to go to a beach house with Sophie and Melissa. I will only give you the shortened version of the trip because it was so good that most of the trip had inside jokes, that no matter how much I try to explain to you, it would not really make sense. We left in the evening on Easter Sunday. We had all decided to spend the morning with our families, so in the afternoon, the three of us met at the airport. As we sat there, the first thing we noticed was, yes, indeed, this was a teacher trip. At our feet, we each had our monogrammed bag. Now, I can tell you without a doubt, there was no alcohol intake on the plane, however, we laughed like drunks. We had so much fun.

The "beach house" was actually in a retirement community and we were by far the youngest people there. Sophie had a connection with some friends who only used it certain times of the year and didn't mind if we used it that week. Many laughs ensued due to the hilarity of the retirement community that we were so unaccustomed to being around. For three days, we enjoyed sandy beaches, wind in our hair, seafood dinners, junk food, window-shopping and good friendship. Three women who had been through our own little versions of hell and divorce were coming together, not to discuss it or dwell on it, but to do something new and fresh, to move past the pain and to be free.

The very first moment I had felt truly free and alive since the horrible thing occurred was on this trip. I was sitting in a chair with the waves crashing on my feet, reading my Escape manual (you know, a girl has to know about her vehicle), with nothing on but a swimsuit. I put the manual down, looked up into the sun and breathed. I truly breathed in contentment and healing. God was so at work in my life. I was truly stepping into myself. I could feel the wind blowing my hair. I knew it was God. In that moment, I had left Melissa and Sophie and I was in a far off place understanding that I truly was okay and the horrible thing was okay, that my children were okay. In that moment, he whispered to me, "You are mine, you are enough, and you are okay."

Later that evening, we went to dinner at a seafood restaurant. This was our "nice" dinner of the week where we splurged on good food. We dressed up and headed out. I think the waves had been tonic for all three of us. The laughs continued throughout the evening. At one point during dinner, Sophie said to me, "Libby, I know you don't know it yet, but you are beautiful." I remember that I didn't know how to take that. It baffled me. It was something that had not been said to me in a very long while, while it was a very sweet statement, it stung just a little because I had not heard such a comment out loud. I'm glad that she was the friend that saw something in me that I couldn't see in myself just yet.

Another friend of mine was also on a vacation with her family in Florida. She also attended the little Presbyterian Church that I was beginning to feel really drawn to. I Facebooked her and asked her for her phone number. At some point while we were both under warm sun, we made a connection on the telephone where I asked her about the church, how I could be involved and some basic foundational questions. After our phone call, I was pretty sure this was my next move. She was so welcoming and it felt good to reconnect with her after all the years. I truly enjoyed reconnecting with old friends. If you haven't noticed by now, I am never one to burn a bridge as I understand there may be a time you will have to re-cross that bridge. This philosophy has served me well in moving back home.

Our week in the sun came to an end faster than we wanted it to. The plane ride back to Shelbyville held three well-rested ladies.

I had a few more days without the girls. I had some time to reflect on the trip. After I was unpacked, Tammy and I met in Louisville on Bardstown Road at what is surely one of my favorite restaurants. Our talks are always so good after we have not seen each other for a while because there is a lot to catch up on and reflect upon. I also caught up with Claire and my family. Spring break 2012 was down in the books.

How quickly the effects of vacations can wear off after a few days of being back in the daily grind. One evening when mom had the girls, I found myself in a place, I quite literally had never been. The sweet little Presbyterian Church had a prayer garden and on this particular night, my heart was very heavy and weighed down. I typically write in a prayer journal, but all I had in my car at the time was a legal pad. I was lamenting the loss of a father in my children's daily lives and to be honest I still felt the loss of a companion in a huge way. One this particular night, I sat down on a concrete slab near a fountain in the prayer garden and furiously wrote on my legal pad my thoughts and fears.

Dear God,

I guess here is as good a place as any just to tell You how confused I am. I hate to say the word confused because I know confusion does not come from You. I guess that, after everything I have been through, there is no better word than confusion. My life at one point felt so together and now it feels so utterly torn apart and I don't know what to do but just depend on You. I feel like I have so many huge tasks in front to of me. I have to take care of my children, first and foremost, and raise them how You would have me bring them up and I don't know how to do what You would have me do. It seems so broken without a father in the home and yet, that is exactly how it is. I know that I am scared of doing it all wrong and I have to trust You completely. I need Your care and help in my life and people who can provide that to me without constraints.

Lord, this church, this very place that I am sitting...Is this Your will and if so, please strike down like lightning and show it to me. I need guidance and direction. I need a place to call mine. I need people to be my people. I need to get an okay from You that I should be here.

I don't know what Your design is for me anymore. I know Your design is best but my heart pleads to be let in on the deal. Lord, You know my heart and the feelings that You designed me to feel and the thoughts You designed me to have. Forgive me for my impatience and urgency. Lord, help me to be patient, but in that patience, find peace. Lord, I need peace.

Beautiful Jesus, would You have me serve here and in what way? Lord, help me make good decisions that cherish my girls and me. Help me rely on You. I commit myself to those desires because anything apart from them is fleeting. Forgive me for my wrongs and my worries. Clarity and peace, I ask for.

Always and Forever,

Libby

Not long after this prayer, I was spending a weekend by myself while the girls were with their dad. It is not often that I sleep in. My body seems to get up early and go. I love the morning time when everything is still and the promise of a fresh new day is before us. On this particular morning, I awakened later in the morning later than usual. It was about nine o'clock in the morning and the sun was creeping through the window. I felt an amazing sense of peace rush over me. I had awakened from a dream. This dream was nothing like the dream of the prehistoric fish in the waters at the Roman Coliseum. This dream was very different and much more assuring. I dreamed that I was sitting in the sanctuary at The Presbyterian Church I had prayed about not so many days before. The sanctuary in this building is filled with stain glass windows and a pipe organ. In my dream, all of the pews were removed and I sat in the middle of the room in a rocking chair with light shining in all of the windows. The warmth that I was dreaming of transferred to my awakened state. In the dream, I was sitting in this rocking chair and in my arms was a newborn baby. This baby wasn't my child, but more like me, holding me and caring for me. The dream was in first person, so as I was sitting there in the rocking chair, holding the baby, the ceiling of the church split open and a direct ray of light shined on to the baby and me. As I transitioned from an unconscious state to alertness, the feeling of love and peace did not leave me.

You can question dreams and the psyche all you want, but when you have an experience such as this, I have found, that if it has some meaning to you, it was real to you. Even if those feelings were created deep within my own inner being, they were attached to a place where I felt love and peace. I had my answer to my prayer. Many times, we do hold the answers to our prayers. When we look deep inside of ourselves, as the dream world allows us to do, we know how we feel or where we should act. Prayer for me has become a deep look at self. God usually provides the answers I need when I look deep into myself. At any rate, even if the situation doesn't change, my attitude or outlook does. That is truly the gift of prayer, it doesn't change the situation, but it does change the believer.

Of course, I am one to over analyze any given situation, a fault most of the time, but I did look up the symbols in this dream and found that I also liked their meanings. To dream about light can be interpreted as being in touch with yourself in a very introspective way. Stained glass windows in dreams represent spiritual healing and enlightenment. The rocking chair symbolized comfort and relaxation. Seeing the sun in your dream represents a strong energy for life. Lastly, to see a baby in your dream symbolizes innocence, warmth and new beginnings.

Often I will look up a meaning of a dream to see how in the world my conscience might have conceived such thoughts and most of the time; dream interpretations make sense, but this particular one met me where I was. It was beginning to be a beautiful time in my life. I was finally feeling free from the horrible thing and all of its ugliness. I was experiencing spiritual healing, I was in touch with myself in a very introspective way, and was finally feeling some comfort in my life. This was my answer to insert my little family into this sweet community of faith at the little Presbyterian Church on the corner of Seventh and Main in downtown Shelbyville. I began to have a church home and a place where I could serve and use talents that God gave me to use for others.

Libby Sears Blair

CHAPTER
THIRTY-ONE

At the same time all of this was stirring in my heart, the end of my first year of teaching was looming overhead. I completed the KTIP program and got the stamp of approval that I was okay to continue teaching in the state of Kentucky. I had agreed to teach summer school that summer. The girls had certain times they were to be with their dad, but he and I worked it out to where he would have them during the time that I taught summer school and I would have them after it was over. There were several things to look forward to. My thirty-fourth birthday was approaching and it was going to be fun, a much better situation than the previous year. I had a lot to celebrate and be grateful for in my life.

I made plans with all of the women who had been ever so present in my life that year and we headed out to a quaint little restaurant in the East end of Louisville that I had known about. The evening was Melissa, Claire, Sophie, Tammy and my Melissa from Hodgenville and her two daughters and I. I sat in a special room in the restaurant encircled by friends and love.

June 2, 2012

Dear Lord,

I do so love waking up this morning and knowing that life is okay. Last year, I cried, as it was my last day of school, my last day of that job, the last day Michael Ray and I would work together and the last of what I knew I was going to be doing. And look WHAT YOU HAVE DONE, what You have given me and what You have provided and look at how blessed I am. New home, new friends, new town, new job, peace in my heart and a smile on my face. You show Yourself to me over and over again. You are in me and all around me and I am forever, ever, ever grateful. Of course I am grateful for Your love and mercy and salvation, but You give me so much more at every turn. Thank You for this life and these blessings. You are amazing God. I feel so free!

And by the way, You know this, but I love my church. Thank You for that gift of direction. May I glorify You in all of my choices.

Love,

Libby

Obviously, my birthday was a truly happy birthday. The summer was looking up to be fun. A trip to Holiday World with the church was a fun event for the girls and a time for me to reconnect and connect with those in my community.

CHAPTER
THIRTY-TWO

I really needed the first year to find my footing and though I was happy, I was still such a newborn into the ways of the world for a single mom. My girls and I had fun at every step, though I admit, there were days that, at the end of the day, there was no more energy left for this momma to keep on going. Ever since the night of the horrible thing, I didn't know the future. One important lesson I have learned is, no matter what, we don't know what the future holds. I think we all would like to say we have dreams and when we put our dreams in motion, that is goal setting, but truly, you can never know what the next day is going to bring. A verse in Proverbs says: "In his heart, man plans his course, but the Lord determines his steps" (Proverbs 16:9, NIV). Though I didn't know the future, I was starting to become comfortable in where I was. I had community, I had friends and I had a place.

There was an old haunt of mine that I had not revisited in the first year because I knew it would beckon me if I opened that door, but one block down from the little church that I had grown to love and adore stood another building that would call to me. I could hear the echoes in my heart as I would drive by it the first year, but I would tell myself, no, you don't have time for that. Shelby County Community Theatre is a gem. It has been running for over thirty years. As a child and throughout high school, I performed on the stage in Shelbyville and this had once been a big part of my life. One thing I know about theatre is that when it calls, and you answer, it can take you in deep. I couldn't resist the yearning much more when one of my friends from long ago was directing a show called "Til Beth Due Us Part" on the local stage. It was one night when the girls were gone and I finally decided it was time to open the door. I called the ticket booth and made a reservation for one.

It was just the same as remembered it. Though I was on the other side, in the audience, I could still feel what backstage looked and felt like. There is a feeling I can't quite describe when you are standing in the dark, quietly waiting for your cue. I am never so in tune with my breathing and my heart rate as I am the moment before I get ready to take the stage. Sitting there, in the dark, I was glad that I had come. I enjoyed the show and the special hometown-feel and touch to the little theatre. It was then, I succumbed and I knew theatre would again be a part of my life. It would be months before I truly became involved but this was the evening that sparked the match.

Summer school came and went. It afforded me more time in the classroom to work on specific reading strategies with kids as well as a little more money in the bank account. When it was time for the kids to come home, I made sure that our days were filled with sunshine and laughter. I bought us summer passes to the local pool that we had frequented the summer before and we spent our afternoons in the water under the sun. Actually, the kids spent most of their time in the water, it was a good time for me to lounge and read as they played. Oh, that the month of July would last longer before school begins.

One particularly hot day, I was in a lounge chair, half reading, half watching the girls and half sleeping when the man next to me and I began to chat. I have no idea how the conversation was started, but it usually doesn't take me long to chat someone up. We began talking all things Shelbyville that led to our discussion of his involvement in Shelby County Community Theatre, which also led to an introduction of another woman at the pool. My now friend, Cyndi Skellie was at the pool and Dan felt that we should be introduced. Within minutes, we were instafriends. Within a matter of days, she and I were making plans to go see movies and go out dancing. She was another single mom and teacher with whom I could share experiences and gain perspective from as well as camaraderie, as we both managed our households independently. The even greater connection was her love for theatre as well as my own, though we had a little age difference; she too had a rich background and connection with the community theatre. We enjoyed laughing, talking and drinking wine.

I had set a personal goal that summer to begin running. I had always wanted to be a runner like my dad, but my short legs and wide hips left me the challenge of it more than the ability to do it. As I said, throughout all of my mental, emotional and spiritual work, I was becoming healthier physically. I didn't drastically change all parts of my lifestyle but little by little, my body wanted healthier things. I gave up sodas altogether for quite some time. I practiced moderation in all things. I truly tried to eat only natural ingredients and stay away from foods with preservatives. My philosophy was this: If it can stay on a shelf for a long period of time, it can stay on your hips as well. And so, in the hot month of July, I signed up for my first 5K. I petitioned Tammy to run with me. It wasn't hard on her as she is naturally inclined to be competitive and a runner. I ran daily. I added the Couch to 5K app to my phone and I would run until the guy said "walk" and then I would walk until the guy said "run". The summer was a leveling out period for me, and the physical activity was such a blessing to be able to do. I enjoyed working up a good sweat and being active. I enjoyed the fact that I was meeting a personal goal. The summer was filled with sunshine, splashes, smiles, laughter and contentment. There was also a huge satisfaction that I had made it through (this part at least).

Tammy and I still had almost daily phone conversations where we talked about budgeting a single household, trying to be three different places at once, as well as our hopes and dreams for the future beyond what we were living in in the moment. I think we both desired partnership. She was in the middle of a relationship that had a lot of navigation attached to it and so we would talk about that. We would talk about where and whom my heart was with at the time. As I am sitting here writing this, I can't think of anything that I have ever hidden from her. I have been completely transparent and open in front her. She has seen the black and the ugly and yet, still answers the phone when I call.

I continued reading through the Bible daily. After reading all of the New Testament, I began reading the Old. Sometimes I struggled with biblical meaning. I think it is okay to struggle with God. In fact, I think it is okay to struggle with anyone, it is when one gives up that it is most concerning. I believe so much in God and God's hand at work that I don't ever want to give up.

CHAPTER
THIRTY-THREE

August 11, 2012

Deuteronomy 6:10

"When the Lord your God brings you into the land he swore to your fathers, to Abraham, Isaac and Jacob- to give you a land with large flourishing cities, you did not build houses filled with all kinds of good things you did not provide, wells you did not dig and vineyards and olive gardens that you did not plant- then when you eat, and are satisfied, be careful that you do not forget the Lord who brought you out of Egypt, out of the land of slavery!"

Lord,

I have enjoyed finally getting to read Deuteronomy. The world that I live in is so far removed from that of the Egyptians and I do know that I have a very difficult time understanding You as a God of Vengeance and Wrath, when in my life, You have been a God of Mercy and Love. Though I don't understand why things happen I still choose to love You.

Lord, sometimes I'm very confused about how to live for You. I'm enjoying reading this scripture because I'm learning so much but it is hard for me to ingest all of the commands and who they were written for. I am not questioning Your authority because I believe with every ounce of my being that You are the Great I Am and that's all I really need to know. I hope that my life and my journey please You. I know I completely rely on You and I want to continue to my whole life. Lord, there are basic principles that I am trying to teach Melody and Anna. Lord, one thing I know is that You are a God of Provision and You don't let me go hungry or thirsty. I praise You whole-heartedly for all the needs you have met in my life and how you have taken me to the land of bread and honey. I know that there are trials along the way and more trials to come but I know it has been done and can be done again.

Please protect my children wherever they are in the world. Help me continue to make good decisions for my children and myself. Help me when I get discouraged. God, please bless Tammy today. Show her the fruits of her labor. Lift her up so that she doesn't feel like she is being drug around. Protect her children everywhere that they are. Thank You for providing her to me as a sister.

Lord, I am in anticipation for what is to come. Help me be a Light to the burdened.

Love,

Libby

September, October and November brought the normal events of the seasons. The ebb and flow of life was returning and we were beginning to get used to our new normal. Tammy and I did a Labor Day Road Trip to Nashville for the weekend. I ran my first 5K with Tammy and was 12th in my age group out of a large volume of people. Melody, Anna and I had our first "family" photo shoot with the three of us. I melted down some old jewelry that Michael Ray had given me and had a ring made with mine, Melody and Anna's birthstones on it. A mutual friend of both Michael Ray and myself baptized Anna. That was a special day as he opened his particular church in Hodgenville for my family and Michael Ray's family to gather without the oddities of having the focus on the broken family in a large audience. The focus was truly on Anna and her decision of faith. Michael Ray and I decided that day that we all must have been doing something right. I moved through feelings about relationships with other men in my life, though I talked with several and set my heart on one, I found that I was still working through the pain of rejection and still healing the innermost part of my heart. God's answer to my desire for companionship was "not yet" and that was okay. It was one of those things that I thought I wanted, but if I had it, I surely wouldn't have known what to do with it, which made me an awkward date or woman to communicate with. I inevitably did it wrong. I began to serve on the Fundraising Committee for the Community Theatre. (I told you! I knew it would happen!) I spent many a Saturday catching up on work or bills at my little coffee shop. Over Fall Break I had gone to meet Michael Ray at his storage unit where he had kept some of our Christmas decorations that we had both owned. I pulled out the things I wanted and came across a bag of little silver bells. They were the same bells that the guests at our wedding rang when we walked into the room as husband and wife. Since Christmas was seven days after our wedding, they were also the only ornaments we had for our tree in 1999. When I saw them, I hesitated. I was overcome with grief and didn't know what to do about them. Something struck me. I looked at Michael Ray and I intentionally took only four of the bells. They represented the family that was Melody, Anna-Kate, Michael Ray and I and it was okay to honor that. I became involved with a ministry called A Place to Sleep and directed my first children's play in Shelbyville. I made my first turkey at Thanksgiving. Tammy and her boyfriend fell away from one another and then reconnected and became closer. Melissa also had found partnership with Martty and on the blink; they decided to have a Christmas Wedding!

Christmas was better and easier this year. I finally had a handle on the new normal, even for the holidays. There was an invitation extended to me to be at Mamaw's for Christmas but I knew my heart well enough to protect it better this year. The girls and I had a beautiful Christmas and enjoyed decorating our little townhouse. I took pride putting the colors of teal and silver and making it truly my own holiday. The anniversary of my wedding came and went much easier. My heart did beat fast when I intentionally hung the four bells on the tree. I think there will always be a little Christmas Past that haunts each of us. The girls were asked to participate in the Christmas service at church. I was bursting with pride. I began to think I was really on the other side of the situation of the horrible thing.

I learned that, sometimes, something would happen that would cause a flood of emotions to arise. Most days, I went on with life as I knew it to be very normally, and then something would occur that would cause a flood of emotions. I learned the craft of taking a moment to deal with what I was feeling, examine it, feel it, respond to it if I needed and then wrap it all back up and put it back on the shelf. My friends and I lovingly refer to this method as "taking the box off of the shelf and putting it back up." Many times we literally do this in life with a box of old letters, pictures or movie stubs. It is the same concept.

CHAPTER
THIRTY-FOUR

I n the second part of the school year, I began contemplating if I should pursue a Rank One to further my education in the area of education. I was considering either counseling or school psychology. I began researching the different degrees and the commitment they would take. I was becoming closer with Chellie, the librarian at school who, as she learned my story, told me that I had a story to tell. Many times, when I would tell people my story from the past year, they would say, "You need to write that down." This memoir is not my own idea as much as it is everyone else's who said it needed to be told. She had written her first book in November of that year and I was in awe of her. She, matter of fact, told me that if she could do it, anyone could do it. Chellie, a sweet, short lady, always had a tremendous smile on her face. She is a very positive cheerleader for anyone who has been through adversity. She gave me this mental image of a swimmer coming up from the water for air, feeling the sunshine on their face. I wish you could hear her melodic voice carry the image. "...and then one day, Libby, you will reach the surface and the sun will be shining on YOU!" She believed it was going to happen for me! She knew the library at West forwards and backwards. One day when we were talking, I explained that I had most everything that was need to be certified in English as well as Special Education. I was mainly saying it in passing. All I really needed was to take the test to be able to teach English. One morning

I walked into my classroom to find the sweetest potted Christmas tree with an encouraging note that said, "Take the PRAXIS!" (The PRAXIS is the test that is required to obtain a certification of a particular content area and I needed to take the test in the Middle and High School English area).

Within a matter of days, the new foundation that I had built for myself would crumble. In terms of my job, I was happy and content teaching seventh grade reading and writing. I would have gladly stayed there until retirement, but my life was to take on a new trajectory. I was following local news consistently and knew that there had been some talk about budget cuts, especially in the Special Education Department. I decided to tackle the news head on and I went to my principal and asked her what she knew. We were standing in the hallway and she opened a computer lab and asked me to come in. I knew then, that she needed a private place to confirm the news that was already in my mind. Yes, it was a budget cut to special education, no the numbers didn't support the position, if I were you I would begin job searching, I will give you a good reference... All I heard was- you are going to lose your job. The foundation that you have built is not strong enough without employment. That is not what she said, but as I processed it, it was the self-talk that I was hearing. Whoever speaks that inner dialogue in my head is dangerous! She reached out and held my hand as I began to sob. West Middle had been my saving grace and I was going to lose it. When I finally could talk, all I could say was "I have lost so much." I felt for her because she was in a position where she had to give bad news that she didn't want to give. I was pretty much shot for the day.

February 23, 2013

Lord,

This is so hard. It has been a very hard week/month. I haven't had a time where my thoughts and feelings were all over the place as much as they are right now in quite a while. Lord, You know all of the ends and outs of what I cannot see. I am hurting and in pain. I am so confused as to what Your plan is for me right now. I feel vulnerable and mad that I have to keep starting over. Not to be presumptuous but I really thought Your plan was for me here at West Middle. They say that there is no guarantee that I will have a job next year, but they think there is a possibility that I will get absorbed into the district. This job is how I take care of my children. I am very scared. Have I not proved to You that I can trust You in all circumstances? God, bad things keep happening in my life. I keep tripping. (This was also said after a conversation with someone who had my heart in the palm of his hand and did not even know it.) Lord, I need a job and I need my heart to settle. Lord, I know my thoughts change every moment, I go from trusting You to not trusting you even though I say I trust You, I go from being scared to being excited, I am confused and worried both at the same time. Ultimately, all human feelings aside, I trust You completely. Thank You for the breath I breathe today. Give me strength to take care of my children when I have no strength. Help me not to mess up. I'm sorry for being mad, I do love You so much. I'm tired of starting over. I do need You so much.

CHAPTER
THIRTY-FIVE

I t took me almost three months before I could be convinced that things would be all right again, somehow, some way. In March, the official word was given that there was absolutely no possibility of me returning to my beloved West Middle. I had a lot of support from my church and my friends. There were days all over again, I found myself going through the motions just as I had done at LaRue County High School when I didn't know what the future held. I tried to hold my head high. I focused on as many positive things as I could. I was pained not knowing how I was going to do it. In a conversation with a veteran teacher, she asked me if I had any other certifications and could possibly teach anything else. I didn't have any other certifications, but I could hear Chellie cheering me on under the noise of life saying, "Take the PRAXIS" and so I did. I signed up to take the PRAXIS.

I then had a focus, something that would keep me going. It was good for me to have a focus. Whenever I have a focus or a goal, outside circumstances don't seem to affect me as much. It was scary to take the PRAXIS as most people take it directly upon graduation. It had been fifteen years since I had an English class in college. I sat down with flashcards every day going over terms according to the *PRAXIS Test for Dummies* guys. Though most of it was a review for me, I felt like everything I had was riding on this test.

I have had a knack, in recent years, to make friends, really good friends with men who are old enough to be my father. Maybe I am naturally drawn to them because I didn't see my own father on a daily basis when I was growing up. I really don't know but these men have been a blessing in my life and have encouraged me beyond belief. One particular man at church always had the right, kind thing to say that would lift my spirits or keep me going. These relationships were one of the many supports that I had during this time. Upon reflection of these relationships, I have always appreciated the breadth of life and experience of these men.

I took the PRAXIS on the last day of state testing for students that year. When they were finished with their test, I left and went to the testing site. I was very prepared. I knew I only had sixty seconds or less to answer each question. I also had an essay question to answer. I was concerned about time and being able to finish the entire test. After being searched from head to toe, to ensure that I didn't have any contraband that would permit me to cheat, I went into the testing room. I had a cubicle, a computer and a pair of headsets I could wear if I wanted to block out the noise. I sat completely still with my hand on the mouse, never moving other than to click the correct response or make a tally mark on a piece of paper if there was an answer of which I was unsure. I knew that I had to answer all but ten questions correctly to pass the test, so when I happened across a question I didn't know, I would make a mark. After answering all of the multiple-choice questions, I had just enough time to answer the essay question. After typing the last word of the response to the essay question, I looked at the timer and it showed 00:00 remaining. I had done it; it was completed. I only had six tally marks for questions I had just guessed the answers. I felt relief.

When I walked out of the testing site, I so badly wanted to share my relief and completion with someone; however, I was alone when I got in my car. I knew I had friends cheering me on, but it was evident to me that I didn't have that special someone to share this type of news with, so I just said a special prayer of thanks for the stamina and the knowledge.

As the end of the school year loomed overhead, I waited patiently for the scores and checked the district website hourly for new job listings and though I had applied for everything I was qualified for, I saw more jobs filled and less posted as we moved closer to summer break. I was beginning to panic.

I knew my two-year stint was up at West and my intention was to go out gracefully. I made a mixed CD for all of my work friends of fun, uplifting songs that I enjoyed. It was my parting gift. It was a time for me to let people know that I had valued their presence in my life and make our parting meaningful. I spent the morning of the last day of school packing up the rest of my classroom and then visiting classrooms to gift people and say good bye. When it was time to leave, I turned in my key and walked out the door by myself. On the drive home, I blared "Defying Gravity" from Wicked out of my car, and I cried as the words spoke for me "I think I'll try defying gravity, and you won't bring me down!" I refused to be brought down by this situation. I had so wanted the last day of school to arrive and to know where I was going to be, but that did not happen. Later that night, Melissa and I had made plans to go out dancing, because in my mind, when all else fails, you can always dance to some funky music. I even talked the DJ into playing "Carry On, Wayward Son" by Kansas. We danced into the night and I was learning that you really are truly all right if you can live in the present.

In Sunday School, at the Presbyterian Church, one Sunday morning, the Sunday School teacher prayed a special prayer for me to find a job and be able to take care of my children. He said, "Lord, we know that you have Libby taken care of. We even pray at this moment for the people that she will be working with and for those who will share a hallway with her." I loved that prayer of positivity. I would later learn how that prayer was answered.

CHAPTER THIRTY-SIX

Before school had let out, I had attended auditions for my first show since the horrible thing had occurred. I had decided that job, or no job, I could benefit from my time and energy being absorbed by my true love, the theatre. I was in! I had been cast as Nurse #2. I was going to be the best Nurse #2 that anyone had ever seen. Claire and I also picked up two yoga classes a week and we continued our running. With the girls being gone every other week during the summer, it was good for me to have plenty to do. After waiting and waiting, I finally received the news that I had passed the PRAXIS, but when I received that news, there were little opportunities left for employment in the district. And I become another year older.

June 5, 2013

Lord,

Things have been a whirlwind. I studied for and passed a test. Perhaps this has opened more doors for me. I have already seen so many doors shut. I'm sitting here this morning with sunburned legs and a touch of a headache. I celebrated my thirty-fifth birthday on Sunday and was able to keep a good perspective about the future on that day, but it was hard. From day to day, I am fearful and get concerned that I don't know how our needs are going to be met. The reality is that my marriage ended. The reality is that I moved here by myself with two little girls. The reality is that I took a job and lost it. The reality is that I am in a new home and just when things got to where I was managing them I lost my footing again and I am so very tired of losing my ground. The reality is that I am lost.

I do have wonderful support and care, but even still, I sit here today, so very discouraged. Even as I do things I love like yoga, running, swimming, theatre, visiting with friends and writing, I don't know what I will be doing come August and at this moment, I really need that peace. You created me as a planner, a provider, a lover and a giver and many of these things I cannot be without a platform on which to do them. Please ease this burden for me.

Amen,

Libby

I don't know why we have to keep learning that our stability isn't in our circumstances; it is in God and who He created us to be. It is so much easier to recognize this truth when fear is not a factor. Many times during this period, I had to remind myself that I need faith over fear and when we, just for a moment falter from faith, we will immediately find ourselves walking in fear.

For whatever reason, the jobs that I had applied for during this time were all filled. I had great evaluations from the previous two years of teaching and now held, not one, but two certification areas and was not able to find a job. Each posting closed and the only thing left was a half time position teaching English (which I now qualified for) and a half time position teaching Special Education. Each one of these positions was at a different location. Desperation can make you come up with all kinds of plans. I decided to see if both of these half time positions could be put together to create a full-time position for me. I called each principal to discuss this possibility. I tried to help them see the benefit of having me. I was desperate and they could probably hear it in my voice. I drove to each school to make myself seen in the flesh and make my pitch. When I went to the high school, I was walking down the hallway with the principal and he explained that this was only a half-time position and I might not want it. I earnestly told him that half-time sounded great to me because I had nothing. Within a few days I interviewed at both places and found that my job concerns would soon be over. I guess that the principals had their own discussions and ultimately, a full-time position had been formed at Shelby County High School in special education teaching resource English. The bonus was that this was my former high school. I was going to teach another year. There were minor changes that had to be made to the girls' school situations and after school care, but the girls were just so happy that I had found a job, they were happy to accommodate. I was so relieved and happy to spend the summer at the theatre literally singing and dancing.

That summer, every day after morning yoga, I stopped by the little coffee shop on the corner of Sixth and Main. The two young college boys who worked there and I got to know each other fairly well over the summer. The day after my employment became official, I came into the shop and the boys were having a random, halfway intellectual conversation as usual. Conversation really could vary from the latest political scandal to the correct way to wear an overcoat or vest. I enjoyed those boys. On this particular day, they granted me the nickname Gamechanger! I loved it. I was pretty heavy into authoring this book at the time and I told them that this story, this nickname and its origin would certainly be told. I then of course felt the need to grant the boys with equally fantastic nicknames. Sam was easy. He is Sam Boomerang and rightfully so, as he can come up with anything rhetorical on the spot, however, Tommy was quite difficult to name. Sam and I decided that there was no nickname for him. He is just Okay. The sarcasm and dancing conversation I had with these boys at any given moment is just another good memory and a highlight of the summer. Deep down I held on to that nickname Gamechanger. The young boys didn't really know the depths of the changes I had experienced, but to me Gamechanger was a victorious name in its own right. I am more fond of this nickname than any other I've ever been granted.

Michael Ray had bought the girls zoo memberships that summer, so the girls and I took many daytime trips to the zoo. We spent many a summer afternoon at the pool. We enjoyed meals of fresh vegetables bought from the local farmers market. In the daytime I worked on furthering and bettering my life and in the evenings, I perfected Nurse #2.

Performing South Pacific at Shelby County Community Theatre was an outstanding experience. I will always view it with the utmost fondness as it drew me back to the stage and the characters that inhabit the work, play, and love that we make. My friend Cyndi was the director of this production and introduced me to so many wonderful people. An honorable mention goes to Corey, who played Luther Billis. I will always and forever count him among my kindred spirits as he and I clicked from the moment we met. There was also Reggie, who played Captain Brackett, who would join the ranks of my older men friends. He has truly been a friend to me since we met in the most creative and artistic of ways. Both men have been motivators in the pure simple sense of the word. Corey is a mail carrier whose dream is to leave Shelby County and be on Broadway. In the meantime, he passes the moments by involving himself in each and every show at SCCT, delivering mail and of course, leaving me sweet little letters in my mailbox. Two more honorable mentions are Reggie's wife Cheryl who sought me out and actively engaged in a lovely friendship complete with handwritten cards with the sincerest remarks and also the sweet and sassy musical director Ms. Lynne who embraced me with open arms and worked with my vocal chords the best she could. We shared hugs, laughs and tears.

The rehearsal schedule was hefty, but welcome due to the thrill of the theatre, the singing, the dancing and the laughter late into the night. When it was opening night, we had all bonded in such beautiful ways. When the show was over, a little bit of our hearts had gone into the South Pacific and I had more people in my core. Community was a huge part of my life.

CHAPTER
THIRTY-SEVEN

Remember Chellie? My champion of writing and the PRAXIS? The one who really encouraged me and told me I could do it? She formed a writing group that summer that I joined. It is another reason why this story is on paper rather than in my heart. She convinced me that this is a story that needed to be told. It was hard to write with all of the ups and downs that life brings, especially when you are telling your own story. I have found, in the process of writing this book, I can really only pour myself into it when I am in a good place mentally. There is so much soul searching and introspective thinking about how I lived my life and the choices I made and how I want you the reader to be able to insert your own horrible thing in where my horrible thing happened. I want you, the reader to see how I didn't give up, even when it seemed hopeless. These are the things that Chellie and I would discuss when talking about the writing process and life in general.

After a fantastic summer of theatre, writing, running, yoga, new friends, visits with family, trips to the zoo, and swimming with my girls, clarity and job placement, it was time for school to start again.

I was to share a classroom with Jennifer. Jennifer had taught at West and so she and I had a lot of mutual friends, which helped bridge the gap from one school to the next. She was wonderful at helping me learn the ropes at my new school. It was perfect because she had firsthand knowledge of where I had come from and where I was going. She and I not only worked well professionally together, but we became friends. She would become my best confidante at school and be a very good advisor for me in all things love and money, which seemed to be somewhat the focus of that period. I was finally starting to become very aware of how to make my money work for me as a single woman and Jennifer was a mastermind at talking through big money decisions with me. At the same time, dating was becoming a normal occurrence in my world and we would discuss the precursors of the date, dissect the date and decide if the man was worthy of any more of my time. Most usually, they weren't. Jennifer was great at giving advice about what to wear (and yes, I began to wear makeup on my dates) and what not to wear. Here is a Jennifer dating tip: Always wear jeans or pants on a first date because you don't want a man to think he has access to what is up there. Yes, it was frank, but I loved her for it.

It was fun being back in my old high school. Though I don't work there now, the year that I spent there was a bit nostalgic and I am glad that I had the experience. Even Cyndi from the Community Theatre taught on my hallway. (Remember that prayer my Sunday School teacher had prayed for the people on my hallway?) I loved how life had a way of coming full circle. Things had settled again and I felt like I was finally coasting the wave, resting if you will, though there was never a time it was not busy. During this time I was writing this book and I began to wonder where the end of the horrible thing was. Sometimes I felt as though I was still in the throes of divorce and other times I felt like such an overcomer. Through all of the times that I had experienced, I still didn't have that closure feeling I wanted to the end of this transition period. It probably would have come sooner if I had not lost my job, but I had to have that experience to know how I would handle things as a single woman. I knew the end of the end of the horrible thing was near.

In October, in service as a board member for the theatre, I helped organize the annual theatre fundraiser, which was a fabulous dinner and auction. One of the auction items happened to be a weekend at a cabin on Dale Hollow Lake. I had done what I could financially to support the theatre and I, in no way was able to make a bid on any of the large items, however, I had friends who were. A bid was made and a sale was final. The cabin weekend had been sold.

CHAPTER
THIRTY-EIGHT

A few weeks down the road, an invitation was extended for me to join Reggie, Cheryl and Dan at the cabin along with many other theatre supporters and lovers. It was easy for me to say yes. I am always "game" as Reggie says. The weekend was to be in January of 2014. The holidays came and went and were not as scary as they had been in the past. I felt like the end was possibly near and this transition that I had been living in the last couple of years would soon be over. I had the opportunity to emcee two very big music shows for Reggie. Creatively, we worked very well together and enjoyed the process.

I spent a lot of time just being the momma I wanted to be to my baby girls. We enjoyed the holidays together. We were beginning our new traditions. Michael Ray and I were truly defining who we were to each other in the aftermath of the horrible thing. I think it is safe to say we are friends who really know each other well.

The beginning of 2014 was very cold. It was the coldest that Kentucky had seen in years. We actually had temperatures in the negatives, not wind-chill factors but actual below zero temperatures. School was out much of January due to snow and cold. We experienced a lot of cabin fever that weekend and I was supposed to spend the weekend at the cabin at the end of the month.

I invited Tammy to go along with me on this trip. Though there had been snow all week, I was still ready to get out. If I was going to have cabin fever, I at least wanted to have it in a different cabin.

Tammy's children and my children both spent the weekend with their fathers, so off she and I went, driving to a cabin on Dale Hollow Lake. Little did I know that this weekend would be the end. I would no longer be the proverbial poster child of divorce, but just a woman making her own path.

We listened to music along the way and shared hopes and dreams as she was now engaged to Scott. The sun was setting faster than we could get there. It was hard to see where we should turn due to the dark sky that loomed overhead. Just when I was completely weary of the drive, I saw electrical lights in the distance and knew we were close. Up and over one more hill, the gravel bumped us along until we saw the cabin, the big huge cabin where we were to stay for the weekend.

Walking into the cabin was a breath of fresh air. I really hadn't seen people in days due to the snow and cold. The cabin had an open layout where the kitchen and large living area connected and many familiar faces from Shelbyville were smiling back at me. Tammy was the perfect companion because she gets along so well with so many people. She and I easily connected with everyone there in no time. Each room in the cabin had a theme. She and I were given the Mickey Mouse room. When we had settled our belongings into the room, we came back upstairs to join everyone in a smorgasbord of food and chats beside the fireplace.

Reggie then announced in true Reggie style that at 8:00 we were all to join him in the master bedroom, if we so chose, for a creative hour. He had driven up before anyone else the day before, so he had an entire day and night in this large cabin with an expansive balcony overlooking a snow covered Dale Hollow. During that time, he had written a short story that he had been charged with for a Christmas publication. Also, in true Reggie fashion, his story was a sci-fi Christmas story complete with robotic alien type creatures and an old fashioned general store. We all joined him in the master bedroom and seated ourselves in a circle on the huge bed and snuggled up to listen to Reggie read his most interesting tale. He invited each of us back the next night to join him again to read from some of our own works. Everyone knew I had been working on a book, but I hesitated to share.

When you write about yourself, you are making yourself very vulnerable. The more honest the writing is, the more you end up revealing your soul and the more you leave yourself open to interpretation and judgment. You have to forsake the worries and the cares of what someone else will think and rest in the fact that your story is yours and not theirs. I was ready, even though I didn't know it, to share the beginning of the end with my friends.

The next day I woke early to a freshly snow covered scenic view of Dale Hollow from the huge open windows in the living area of our cabin. I felt so alive and well. With a blanket wrapped around me, my hands holding a hot cup of coffee, I stood, looking out the window at the snow quietly falling to the ground, thankful for the moment. As everyone began to rise, we noisily began preparing a big breakfast for all to enjoy. A hike was planned for those that wanted to for later in the day and if we wanted to sit in our pajamas all day that was okay too. Later on, several of us had layered up and set out to go down to the bottom of the hill that would reveal a frozen lake. It was not something I had really seen before. I was completely in tune with myself and the nature that surrounded me. When Tammy and I got back from the hike, after eating, we decided to get in the big hot tub that was out on the deck. The sprint through the snow to the steamy water was tough but worth it, as we plunged all of our bodies but our heads into the water. Snow encircled us as we sat there laughing. I remembered thinking about the beginning of my journey, after the horrible thing began, with a cabin where I cried my eyes out and drank Nyquil to attempt two hours' worth of sleep. I told her, in that hot tub as we puffed on flavored cigars, I thought it was the end of the end.

That night, I read the beginning of my story for those who dared to come back for another of Reggie's creative hours in the master bedroom. I received feedback and encouragement that the story had meaning and should be told. And, so, I am telling this story to you dear reader, not for focus on me, but for focus on hope and joy.

The next morning, I spent some time by myself reading in Psalms 30. It coincided with my life so much that I posted it on Facebook.

The post read: You did it! You changed my wild lament into whirling dance; You ripped off my black mourning band and decked me with wild flowers. I'm about to burst with song; I can't keep quiet about you. God, my God, I can't thank you enough. (Psalm 30:11, The Message). When I walked upstairs, Cheryl was sitting by the fire perusing Facebook and she said to me, "Libby, I've got it. I know the name of your book. The Whirling Dance." With my heart swollen, I agreed.

When Tammy and I loaded up the car to head back, I realized we would be travelling near where my Grandmother was in her assisted living home. As her 89th birthday was the next day, it was nice to stop and visit with her and my mom who was also visiting her. On that day, she wasn't sure who I was, but I was bright and brim with life thoughts that swam around in her head. She recited for us this day part of Henry Wadsworth Longfellow's Poem "Psalm of Life". She said:

Life is real; life is earnest!

And the grave is not its goal;

Dust thou art to dust returnest,

Was not spoken of the soul.

Not enjoyment and not sorrow,

Is our destined end or way;

But to act, that each tomorrow

Find us further than today.

Now, Grandma might not have been able to talk to us and tell us how she felt about an 89th birthday, but she certainly has some words of wisdom for me as I was reaching the end of a journey and starting a new one.

We met Michael Ray to pick up my girls in Elizabethtown and I drove Tammy on to her home. As I stepped foot into my little townhouse, I had been transformed by the renewing of my heart. I knew I was onto something new. Not that something new is better. It also has its learning curves as I walk this world as a single woman who is not settling for just anything, a mother who ferociously cares for her children, a professional who desires to be rooted and a child who wants to play.

I have since lost and found another job due to that whole "reduction in force" thing. I still mess things up daily. My heart is open to what God gives me. I walk in faith and not in fear. When things are hard, I have this period in my life in which to reflect. I know and can say that I will be okay. I am strong. I survived the whirling dance. I now know the whirling dance and dance it well, for it is a part of me and all glory goes to God who gave me this beautiful, messy life.

*Please forgive any paraphrases or non-cited scripture references as most all that is shared was part of a personal journal.

Made in the USA
Middletown, DE
22 March 2016